A Raven's Gift

Foreword

Bryan Hupperts has a way with words! His sometimes light-hearted and even funny word-pictures have a way of disarming the reader, and before you realize what is happening you find that the *"ouch"* words have gone into your heart and changed some things.

The stories contained in this little book are real-life word canvases that anyone can relate to. The tender-hearted way that Bryan can "get to you" makes his parables easy to receive. This is the way Jesus often spoke to His disciples. There is a life-giving lesson in every chapter and each chapter is autonomous. I recommend one-a-day - like a vitamin. This is not a heavy book, but it describes serious issues that affect us all. Bryan manages to shoot (without a lot of blood-shed) some, *"Little foxes that spoil the vine, for our vines have tender grapes"* (Song. 2:15).

Kathie Walters,
Author
Good News Ministries

Acknowledgements

This book, the first in a series, is a labor of love that has spanned many years. While our influencers have been many, we would especially like to thank the many individuals that have helped support, love and keep us sane!

Our love goes out to Tom and Mary Helbig, our pastors, and our church family at World View Community. To our graphic artist Jack Whitney, thanks for your creativity; to our family in Australia, Storm-Harvest Ministries, which consists of Rob and Kellie Homes, Brian and Angela Grewel, and last but not least, the Liu family, thanks for your many prayers and your friendship.

With loving acknowledgement, Mr. & Mrs. Leong in Malaysia, for your prayers, love and support, and for letting me marry your daughter! To the entire Hupperts clan, especially my brother David, our computer guru, see *Turk or Porky*, page 53, and our two adorable children, who have been wellsprings of inspiration, David and Amber Jade, thanks for putting up with the book birthing process.

Finally, to the cashew chicken queen, my editor-in-chief, my lovely wife Cyndi, your deepsheep would simply like to say, *"ba-aa."*

Table of Contents

Gizzards and Other Slimy Stuff

I meandered into a supermarket keeping my marriage secure by accompanying my wife while she shopped. Successful husbanding often calls for sacrificing Saturdays on the altar of family service. All was well until we hit the frozen foods aisle. This store was having a special on whole chickens and, budget conscious family that we are, we decided to stock up. A raw bird in the freezer is worth more than a bucket with biscuits from KFC on the table –and it costs a lot less.

As I walked down the aisle, I saw frozen dead bird after frozen dead bird each with its plucked backside turned upward facing me. Each lay there dead in its own frozen dignity. I was undecided if this was a coincidence or if these birds were being allowed to fire off one final salvo at the entire cruel chicken-eating world. Unless you are poultry or are a poultry sympathizer, the whole scene was brutally comical.

Having only considered chickens by their parts and not their feelings, I got an eerie case of the willies when I realized that I was standing in what amounted to a dead chicken morgue. I started feeling foul for these deceased birds. Fortunately, my wave of guilt-stricken empathy gave way to my more practical nature in the guise of hunger pangs. I popped a few chicken corpses into our cart and off we went.

When we got home we decided to thaw one of the birds out and have it for dinner. After it thawed for a few hours, I was given the unceremonious task of skinning the bird. That's when I found the bag of gizzards and other slimy stuff inside.

I reached inside the chicken's semi-frozen featherless flesh and pulled out a bag of spare parts. Now this has happened to me when working on cars and appliances - I'm a guy so no problem - but from a chicken? If this had been a grab-bag game, I would have figured that I had just lost. Breasts, legs, thighs and drum-sticks, okay; but gizzards?

I am not even sure what a gizzard does. I looked up *chicken parts* on the Internet, but all I could find were chicken recipes. Save for Southern cooking, I couldn't find even one recipe that called for gizzards.

As I began to dismember the bird, I found myself thinking about the body of Christ. The Psalms do say that He'll cover us with his feathers and wings! Chickens are bred to lay eggs and/or to be eaten. Poultry have a destiny that reaches no higher than my fork. It is not so with the church of the Lord Jesus Christ.

A body divided against itself cannot stand. When we are divided, as they say, parts is parts. When I found myself looking at the components that make up a chicken there in little lifeless piles of pieces on the cutting board, I suddenly understood the devil's classic strategy to wage successful war on the Body of Christ: divide and conquer.

There is a mystery and an impartation of life that takes place when Christians work with and serve one another. The hand cannot say to the eye, *"I have no need of you."* Just ask the chicken where she would be without her gizzards; probably in serious pain. And God delights to give "less honorable" parts greater honor.

Here are some tasty Truths I learned from my dinner and the Bible. 1 Corinthians 12:14-27 — *"For the body does not consist of one member but of many... But as it is, God arranged the organs in the body, each one of them, as he chose. God has so composed the body, giving the greater honor to the inferior part, that there may be no discord in the body... Now you are the body of Christ."*

A chicken is greater than its individual parts. Gizzards are important, but so are drumsticks. And preachers are important, but so are givers and intercessors. Whatever part God has given you in His church, be that. We cannot live out the corporate life of Christ here on earth without all being in community with each other, each one doing our God-ordained part.

Gizzards, those people we seldom see but miss when they're not functioning, are a grace gift to the church. I am not holding up a lowly standard of fleshly unity, but the high and holy standard of True Unity. We, the body of Jesus Christ on this earth, need each other so that we can fulfill the race we were individually given to run. A soul winner needs givers and prayer warriors to help support the task of soul winning. Givers and prayer warriors need soul winners to be their legs and voice to share Christ with the lost. The body needs pastors to nurture and care for new converts.

The kingdom of God is never a solo gizzard, one-man show. But if the gizzards don't gizz, then who will?

If we labor together, each with our gifts being used in the proper place, we all win. And if not, we end up lifeless chicken parts on the kitchen cutting board of hell. A chicken who forsakes assembling together is just a pile of dysfunctional, dismembered poultry parts. The truth is, parts need parts!

The Dentist

My tooth is hurting and I have to see my dentist immediately. I have been putting this dreaded visit off for some time. Alas, the day of reckoning is upon me. The thrill of the drill awaits.

Years ago I injured my jaw in a swimming accident and chipped a few teeth. It isn't noticeable to the unaided eye but, on cold Midwestern mornings, it is still painful. While enduring dental surgery I learned something from my dentist about the God who designed this universe.

The root in my tooth was dying and I needed a root canal done quickly. My mouth was bleeding profusely. I gagged the word through my dry, unresponsive, Novocained lips, "*Uggghhhh?*" Translation: "*Why am I bleeding like a stuck pig in a slaughterhouse?*"

He understood my gurgles and he answered, "*You're bleeding because your body is trying to save the dying nerve in your tooth. Your body is rushing all available blood to the tooth to save it. Now spit.*"

Our bodies have enough sense to know that only by applying the blood can you save something that is dying. Life is indeed in the blood.

Like my patron saint Job, that which I feared has come upon me. I must face the dentist whose visits and pleas to see me via colorful cartooned postcards I have ignored. I will sit in that chair, have my mouth forced open, and let a man drill into my bone structure while lecturing me on making regular dental visits. I will not be in a position to argue or even reply. I will take all he dishes out and then, the crowning indignity - I will write him a hefty check for the trouble.

I will stare into the eyes of the unsmiling receptionist I have been avoiding and schedule a follow-up visit. Knowing my history, she'll put her black pen down and write my appointment lightly in pencil while slow-burning a menacing glare at me. I will then leave and be forced to suck cold soup through a straw for lunch and drool uncontrollably in public till the painkiller wears off.

I would ordinarily find a way out of this, but today I am looking forward to that which I fear. Why? I want the pain to stop. I want to smile again freely, not in a pained grimace that suggests that I am plotting to kill someone. Yes, I feared my dentist. Today, I want his touch because only he can make all things new in my mouth.

We often see God in this same contorted light.

Often we run blinded by fear when we have failed and are in need of mercy. We look at Him like the big mean dentist in the sky who will operate with a rusty crowbar on our wounded, bleeding soul - alas, no Novocaine provided. We gotta suffer a bit first! When we've whimpered and groveled before Him enough, well then, okay. Then He'll dole out the grace, slap a dirty Band-Aid on our festering wound, and get us on our undeserving way.

This is God according to all the bad press He gets. It is not a real picture of Him at all. He convicts, to bring repentance. He chastises, to help His kids grow up to be responsible. He judges, to bring correction. He is ruthless against sin, because sin kills and He wants us to live!

The next time the Lord begins to convict you about something, heed the warning. Respond before the pain begins. It's better to be laid out before his altar for a bit of godly chastening than finally being laid out under his knife needing major oral surgery. If I had gone for the filling when the problem was small, I wouldn't need the root canal.

Daddy's Surprise Visit

One night I put my kids to bed, let my wife have an overdue evening off to curl up undisturbed with a book, and I finished the dinner dishes and was getting ready to shut our home down for the night. And I suddenly felt the Presence of the Lord descend upon my home beckoning me to come outside. I put up the dishrag, quietly opened the front door, and slipped outside into the darkness. It was one of those glorious nights when you can see to the edge of forever. The air was cool and there was a divine kind of silence that seemed to fill the skies.

And then there was the Cloud of His Presence hanging like an intoxicating perfume over my driveway. It felt as if I were being caught away, like the prophets of old who walked with God. Perhaps it would be more fitting if we called His second coming the Enrapture rather than just the Rapture. It is more in keeping with his character and beauty. Heaven seemed close, the stars seemed to bow low, and the Spirit of God permeated everything. His Presence seemed to animate the grass and trees with an overflow of the essence of Life.

I found myself summoned into the Presence of God, and I joyfully accepted the invitation. Like King David, I danced and leapt in utter abandonment praising the Living God on sacred, holy ground that a moment before was only asphalt. There was a rhythm of movement in that moment that lacked the flow of time, yet it was perfect rhythm, were the trees and fields clapping their hands?

And I raised my hands to the skies in celebration and began to weep and shout and laugh all at once for the glory of His Presence. Poetry and praise, psalms from my soul, ran from my lips flowing freely like a waterfall. All within me burst forth in praise to my Redeemer. And in the stillness of that moment, in the recesses of my inner being, I knew He was God.

I felt so small. He seemed so great.

And then time began to move again as the Presence of the One who inhabits eternity began to wane. In the afterglow as He began to withdraw I could feel my heart beating. There was a light everywhere that cast no shadow and flowed more like a fluid than a beam. It surrounded everything like running water until all was saturated with the Presence of God. I was immersed in Him. It was like a baptism, not into his death like water baptism, but into the essence of His Life!

In the language of the Spirit, there were no words spoken, no revelations or insights of truth, just a brief unveiling in my heart of God as He truly is in the stunning beauty of His holiness.

All was again quiet, and the stars were again shining, and the glory cloud withdrew. I had not been transfigured like Christ on the mountain - just transfixed with His burning glory. It was like falling in love all over again.

No one can see the face of God and live - yet no one can really live until he has been touched by His hand. Greater than the shadows cast by the Law, Moses knew God face to face - and now we, because of greater grace, can know Him heart to heart.

And as I turned to go back inside a verse of Scripture spoke the Truth of that moment to me. Genesis 3: 8 — *"And they heard the sound of the LORD God walking in the garden in the cool of the day."*

The God of all Creation had come down to spend a few moments in the twilight of an otherwise unremarkable day to enjoy the company of one of His sons. And I realized that it was just past Father's Day and my Daddy came for a surprise visit.

I went back in the house and kissed my children and wife a sweet good night.

Loving Precious

I was once privileged to lead a youth group to do a three-day Vacation Bible School. On the third and last night, I had the distinct impression to really wait upon the Lord during the ministry time. After the singing and testifying of the goodness of loving Jesus was over, the Spirit of God began to come in a way the Quakers of generations ago called, *"the felt Presence of the Lord."*

Our team lined up in front and we invited children and adults to come forward for prayer. After a bit, a white woman came forward holding a little black girl who couldn't have been more than six months old. And when the child's face was turned towards me, I stood there stunned by her disfigurement.

Her head was grossly misshapen and bore the marks of major corrective surgeries. Her mouth was the wrong shape, more like an oval, where she placed her hands. Her fingers were grouped together on one hand giving her actually only three functioning digits. And her eyes were the most tragic: they were a good two inches apart, not crossways, but vertically. And one of them appeared to lack an iris, giving the impression of severe cataracts.

The foster mother brought the baby forward for prayer. It was obvious from the look on her face that she deeply loved this misshapen girl. She explained that the baby was the victim of severe birth defects - her mother had unsuccessfully tried to abort her - and that she was praying, asking God for the privilege to adopt this baby and raise her as her own daughter.

For a moment, I was so overcome with shock I hesitated to pray. And the volunteer mother stunned me further by announcing the baby's name: Precious. My beautiful Malaysian wife Cyndi's Chinese name is Poe Yoke, which means Precious

Jade. My wife is named Precious, too.

While praying for this little girl, the Holy Spirit convicted me of a truth too painful to ignore. I had been bewildered by her twisted appearance because she didn't look *normal*. Suddenly, I saw the human race, myself included, before a Holy and Perfect God. He seemed to whisper, "*Bryan, you have no idea how mangled and disfigured you are because of the effects of sin. Your birth defects are in your soul. Despite your deformed twistedness, I love you freely. And this child will teach many to love. Now love her.*"

I called to two of our student leaders to pray for Precious while the Holy Spirit touched this baby girl whose needs touched me so deeply. And I realized that God's love covered a multitude of my sins. He sought me out, a refugee on a fallen planet, a deformed, misshapen alien child, and He loved me freely.

All that seemed grotesque in me He kindly looked beyond in order that He might heal me and give me His kingdom. I think I finally saw why some come to Christ and others do not - and I will not enter into a predestination argument with anyone - some want to be adopted and some do not. It's a choice.

God promises healing for the entire Creation. One day, according to Isaiah 35:6, "*Then shall the lame man leap like a hart, and the tongue of the dumb sing for joy. For waters shall break forth in the wilderness, and streams in the desert.*" God's unfathomable love will heal a universe that has been twisted and deformed by sin. On that great day, according to Zephaniah 3:19, God says, "*I will save the lame and gather the outcast, and I will change their shame into praise and renown in all the earth.*"

Where some would only see a deformed baby who "should have been aborted for her own good," God sees a Princess, a regent, who shall one day rule and reign with Him in righteousness. Often, those people that we discard, or walk by and never quite see, those who are different, God sets them aside and names them Precious.

Desert Blossoms

Deuteronomy 8: 2 — *"And you shall remember all the way which the Lord your God has led you in the wilderness (desert) these forty years, that he might humble you, testing you, to know what was in your heart, whether you would keep his commandments or not."*

The dry times, those painful seasons of barrenness, are times to be humbled before the Lord. Jesus said that the Father was glorified when we bore *"much fruit that remains."* Notice when the children of Israel finally got fruit: after they had walked through the desert. Fruitfulness is the ultimate objective of God for you when He has you walking through a desert.

What is precious in the desert? Sand? No, there is shifting sand everywhere. Sky? No, in fact, there is little protection from the merciless beating of the sun. What is precious in the desert is water.

Water can make the difference between living and dying. Water is the precious commodity of life. Most plants cannot survive in deserts. For those that can, survival depends on their taproot digging deep through the sand to find water. Having water is the decisive factor between what lives and what dies.

Look at the history of God's dealings with his saints. He led His people out of Egypt by the hand of Moses, through the desert and to the Promised Land. John the Baptist lived in the desert until God made his ministry public. Jesus was *led by the Spirit* into the desert to be tested by the devil. Paul spent years in the desert before his commissioning as an Apostle. God has used the drought of many deserts to forge some of His finest saints.

Deserts are such obscure places. They precede blessing but are themselves looked upon as curses. They function to bring you to the place of having to only concern yourself with the basics of existence. It is when water, symbolic of the Living Word of God, becomes the only issue of your life, what you live and die by, are you finally ready to enter into the Master's service. When all else in this world appears as sand in your eyes, empty barren waste, you are ready for Kingdom service.

Deserts have the curious effect of hardening your resolve while humbling your heart before God.

Plants grow in direct relation to the amount of water available. When you can blossom with just a little water, you can blossom anywhere! After the desert, you will be thriving "like a tree planted by the water!"

Plants that survive the desert have root systems that can find water. The roots' absorption force must be greater that that of the soil. In other words, you have to thirst more for the Waters of Life than the world. It is when you hunger and thirst for righteousness that you are satisfied.

Don't curse the desert times. God is testing you, seeing what is in your heart. Actually, He is letting you see what He has seen all along. Allow your roots to grow deep into God so that *"out of your belly shall gush forth rivers of living water."* A river in the desert suddenly springing forth? Sure, that's His way.

God often uses the desert to prepare the messenger. When the messenger is ready, then the message comes. We have our part to prepare ourselves for the ministries God calls us to. We also have to be prepared by God for those same tasks. When we can serve Him in a place of barrenness, we can serve Him in a place of fruitfulness. When we are humbled and broken of our own power, then God can show Himself strong on our behalf.

There are some beautiful things growing in the desert. Be patient and let Him finish what He has started in you. It takes a deep, well-developed root system to be able to not only nourish a plant, but to produce and feed the growing fruit on its branches. If there are no roots, there will be no fruit. And His goal is to bring you to a place of fruitfulness, for the Father is glorified when we bear much fruit.

A Raven's Gift

Ravens often appear in Scripture as God's unlikely servants. They are officially listed as *unclean* birds - untouchables - yet they have performed wonderful service to God and His people. Ravens are often God's unlikely resource bringers when times are tough. So what exactly is a raven in the kingdom of God?

A raven is a creation of God. Ravens are often people who look different, think different, act different, people who just don't quite fit into any special social molds. Musicians are often a kind of raven. They're well ... musicians. Seriously, ravens are unlikely people, often not even Christians, that God brings into your life to bless you - and you get to be a witness for Christ to them.

The Old Testament had to do with external things while the New promises the substance, the reality of the kingdom, that is placed in our hearts. In Leviticus 11:15, God proclaims a list of officially banned birds including, *"Every raven according to its kind."* God calls eating these birds *"an abomination."* They are declared off limits, not to be touched, and unclean.

You'd think God would have declared an official raven hunting day to rid the planet of these dark, often course, birds. But no - they are under his special provision and protection! Why? Simply because He loves them.

Unclean ravens are under the blessing of God. He cares for them and feeds them. Luke 12: 24 — *"Consider the ravens: they neither sow nor reap, they have neither storehouse nor barn, and yet God feeds them."*

It is in moments of utter need that ravens seem to show up. The Old Testament Prophet Elijah was running for his life. He had no where to turn, no friends to help him, and he was out of options. God told him to run to a certain brook and said that he had commanded the ravens to feed him.

1 Kings 17: 4 - 6 — *"'You shall drink from the brook, and I have commanded the ravens to feed you there.' So he went and did according to the word of the LORD; he went and dwelt by the brook Cherith that is east of the Jordan. And the ravens brought him bread and meat in the morning, and bread and meat in the evening; and he drank from the brook."*

The land was in severe famine yet Elijah lived many days off of the provision the ravens brought. The ravens provided a temporary source of food for him. Without those ravens showing up morning and night with bread and meat, he would have starved. Birds of prey don't normally share, but when it is God who commands them, they can become the source of great blessing. Those unclean ravens must have been more welcome than any beautiful bird in the sky, more beautiful than the soaring eagles – because they were actually helping this needy prophet!

A friend of mine was a missionary in Haiti, and returned home destitute, penniless, and in great material need. He and his family ended up on food stamps for a short time until they could get back on their feet financially. They kept declaring *"God's elect do not beg for bread,"* until they finally humbled themselves and recognized the food stamp offer as God's raven. It was a temporary blessing that they felt was unclean, yet it got them through the want of the moment.

The truth about the blessing of ravens is expressed perfectly in Job 38:41. *"Who provides food for the ravens, when its young ones cry to God, and wander about for lack of food?"* The ravens may be the delivery boys, but the real source of provision and blessing is really God himself.

It takes genuine humility to see beyond the *uncleanness* of the raven and perceive the hidden hand of God. Many of King

David's mighty men were listed among the unclean.

It was God himself who commanded the ravens to bring provision the prophet and He may well command unclean people to be a blessing to you in your time of desperate need. Look beyond the visages of the strange people about you, that boss with the purple hair, that foul-mouthed meat cutter who blesses you with extra cuts, that God-hating professor who helped you get a scholarship. They're ravens sent from God to bless you in your time of need.

Use eyes of faith and look beyond the offense of the raven and you'll behold the secret blessings of God. When it seems that hope is lost, lift up your eyes and watch for a raven. He is sent to you from God.

Dances With Spears

There was an award winning movie released not long ago called *Dances With Wolves*. Occasionally, even Hollywood gets something right. The film title was taken from the given Indian name of a lone white soldier stationed at an obscure outpost who befriends a wolf. It looked to the Indians as if this soldier was dancing with the wolf when he played with it and tried to feed it from his hand. He was given an honorary name to describe his actions.

Long ago, there was another soldier named David and he danced a very dangerous dance - with spears! David had a problem: God's favor rested on him. That would be a blessing were it not for the fact that God's hand of judgment was against the sinning leader, King Saul. And the more God blessed David the deeper Saul's rage went until he was reduced to being a volcanic vent of reasonless, hellish fury. Finally, in a fit of blind madness, Saul tried to pin David to a wall with his spear.

The irony in this story is that there was a time when Saul had offered David his personal kingly armor to wear when he faced the giant Goliath of Gath. King Saul once looked upon David as a son and even offered his daughter to him in marriage in order to adopt him as a son. That same spear that Saul hurled at David in an attempt to murder him was in all probability part of the King's armor.

Never accept the favors of a man who has incurred God's disfavor. They come with hidden, exorbitant interest charges. A blessing that an ungodly man can give you will often corrupt into a deadly curse and snare. Some free things just end up costing too much. A man who has scorned the fear of God has only his hellish nightmares left to console him. A double-minded man is unstable in all of his ways.

The Bible recounts this story: 1 Samuel 18:10 -11 — *"And on the morrow an evil spirit from God rushed upon Saul, and he raved within his house, while David was playing the lyre, as he did day by day. Saul had his spear in his hand; and Saul cast the spear, for he thought, 'I will pin David to the wall.' But David evaded him twice."* Here we have a demonized king raving in his house. He stalked his own palace corridors screaming at echoing, taunting voices no one else could hear. This fallen king was a howling, murderous madman.

And what was going on behind the scenes? Jesus said, in John 10:10 *"The thief comes only to steal and kill and destroy."* The sworn enemy of God and man, the devil, is at work. He tries to steal, or kill, or destroy you. And the devil had found a most willing vessel in mad King Saul. We are commanded to be filled with the Spirit, and when Saul rejected God's ways, he was filled with a spirit, but not the Holy Spirit of God.

As Bob Dylan once said in a more lucid moment, *"You gotta serve somebody."* Remember that David had earlier rejected the king's armor when he faced Goliath. Why? Because long before he had already chosen to wear the triumphant armor of Light! The Lord himself was his shield and strength. David obeyed Ephesians 6:11 *"Put on the whole armor of God, that you may be able to stand against the wiles of the devil,"* millennia before it was actually penned.

Now what do you do when the king has regally chosen you for target practice? Do you pick up the spear and fight back or walk away? David didn't declare a personal war on Saul and he refused to fight him. All through the rest of King Saul's sad life, David honored him. He even avenged his death and wrote him a requiem that remains the perhaps the sweetest, saddest song in the Bible describing the insane king as, *Lovely.*

And God made David King and he ruled the Golden Age of

Israel. When the battle really belongs to the Lord, the victory is ultimately His. David didn't take the spears that were hurled at him and throw them back. He left his place of honor, his friends, and his reputation behind and walked away and let God fight for him.

Deep suffering both formulates and reveals character. Either you become bitter and vengeful, or it drives you fully to God in total soul surrender. In the breaking process you become His worshipper. Who could have ever imagined that the spears that threatened David's life would instead become the doorway to blessing?

Funny thing about that spear. Saul carried it with him as he hunted through caves and hills trying to find David so he could kill him. And lo! The Lord delivered this spear-toting king into David's hands. David found the king and his guards sleeping. And what was lying next to him stuck into the ground? 1 Samuel 26:7 — *"There lay Saul sleeping within the encampment, with his spear stuck in the ground at his head."*

David took the spear that was nearly the instrument of his own death and went quietly away into the night. This is such a powerful scene because it meant that God had taken away the enemy's power to hurt David. And David feared God more than he feared his mortal enemy. David called out to Saul and told him that he could have killed him but he had shown him mercy and Saul sent one of his men to retrieve his spear from David. And Saul did not ever hunt for David again.

Shortly after this incident, Saul faced his real enemies in battle and he lost. And if David were still his General he would have surely prevailed. But insane men have a way of driving away those very people that God sent to bless and strengthen them. Without David at his side, Saul finally lost the war.

Interesting that Saul was *"badly wounded by the archers."* In other words, the enemy shot him through with tiny arrows - spears - until he was too weak and wounded to move. But then, *"Vengeance belongs to God. He will repay."* Rather than be captured in battle, Saul committed suicide by taking his own sword, another kind of spear, and falling upon it.

Go ahead and dance with the spears, but leave the spear-throwing to the madmen and let God fight your battles. He is a sword and shield to those who greatly fear Him.

Stinky Diapers and Colicky Babies

I'll never forget the wonder and awe-inspiring joy I felt when my son David was born. It was an exciting, messy experience that will live with me forever. I assumed that having a baby made me a Dad. The reality of dadhood hit home a few weeks later when I had to change my first loaded stinky diaper.

Our son was born with respiratory problems and was on antibiotics. This resulted in runny stool that seemed to know intuitively just where the weak points in the diaper liner were. I saw the need to call Cyndi to come help *her* baby. She yelled back that she was cooking dinner and that I should do it myself.

She was in the kitchen plotting this vilest of moments. I could have sworn I heard a low, dark, manic giggle slowly bubbling in the background. I dismissed it. I mean, why would she be smirking?

I'm a new millennium kind of man so no problem. I laid my beautiful son on the changing table and opened his diaper. Nothing in life could have prepared me for that disgusting, defining moment.

That gagging smell! Cruelty, thy name is Mommy.

I nearly choked. I was gasping for clean air in a "God, help me, please" sort of way. The "load of stuff" leaked all over me, all over the table, all over everywhere. It seemed to have a life of its own. What a disgusting sensory overload! Putrid would come close to describing the overpowering, pungent aroma emanating from the inside of that diaper. I don't know what was greener, my face or "it."

I cried out for help to my wife who was having an evil chuckle at my expense, leaning against the kitchen counter gasping for breath from her erupting peals of laughter. She knew what was going to happen! This was a crude demonstration of squaw humor at its lowest.

I received the rite of baptism and officially became a father in that awkward moment. Sure, it's funny now... but then? No way.

I relate this story to make a point. My wife and I were discussing a problem we see in the church regarding new converts. We can win people to Christ but have a dismal record in keeping them in the church. We have been trying to understand where we, the church of the Lord Jesus Christ, have been failing. Many churches will welcome *transferred growth* (people who are already believers) but readily ignore and neglect new babies in Christ. This is tantamount to spiritual child abuse. The problem is pandemic crossing all denominational lines.

I came from a denomination that had several wonderful core values that I still hold to. They include worship, simplicity, and unity (but NOT at the expense of Truth). As I look back, I realize that we, and most the rest of the Western Christian world, lacked one overriding core value: a genuine value of people.

People, especially new babies, are an inconvenience. They make nasty messes and need lots of care and someone to keep them clean. Are they worth the bother to you? Diapers and colic can be both disgusting and frustrating. Babies are a life-time investment that generally only yield long-term results.

Would you order a newborn to change his own diaper? Would you tell him that if he's hungry, go feed himself? No, not unless you were prepared to face criminal child neglect charges. Babies need adults to care for them because they cannot do it themselves. This is God's plan. New converts, i.e., babies in Christ, are in the same situation.

Where are the fathers and mothers in the church? Our babies are dying from neglect not because of abuse, but because of apathy. It's apparently too much trouble to care for them. A new babe is born into your church, takes your churches' name, and then goes public with a stupid stunt. What do you do? Redemptively parent them or show them the door and publicly disavow any knowledge of them?

We need to see people in the light of the plan of Redemption. Christ came into this world to save sinners. He committed unto us the ministry of reconciliation.

We are to go in His name and save sinners, too. Once they're saved, we need to help clean them up, feed them, and help them grow in Christ. We gotta change their soiled diapers and love them at the same time.

An unchanged diaper leads to diaper rash. If it continues unchanged, it can lead to infection, disease and finally death. Someone has to soil their clean hands and change the diapers.

Will it be you?

Three Kinds of Fire

Leviticus 6: 13 — "(HOLY) *Fire shall be kept burning on the altar continually; it shall not go out.*"

Leviticus 10: 1-2 — "*Now Nadab and Abihu, the sons of Aaron, took their respective firepans, and after putting fire in them, placed incense on and offered STRANGE fire before the Lord, which He had not commanded them. And Fire came from the presence of the Lord and consumed them, and they died before the Lord.*"-

Malachi 1: 10a — "*Oh that one among you would shut the gates, that you might not kindle USELESS fire on my altar.*"

Fire in scripture is a powerful image used in a number of ways. God is called a Consuming Fire. Like fire, He consumes all that is not consistent with His nature. Fire burns and gives light. It is a symbol of the glory of the Lord.

Fire is used in war as a signal, it is used to offer sacrifices, and it gives light in the darkness. God appeared as a pillar of fire by night to give light to the Israelites. Fire speaks of the holiness of God. He gives fire to believers like on the day of Pentecost when tongues of fire appeared on the disciples. He will give fire to unbelievers on the day of Divine retribution in the lake that burns with fire.

Under the Old Covenant, it was the responsibility of the priest to keep the fire that God ignited from heaven kindled and burning. It is our responsibility as kings and priests of the New Covenant to keep the fire of faith burning brightly inside.

There are three kinds of fire in scripture. Holy fire, strange fire, and useless fire. Holy fire is offered in our hearts when the people of God are each walking in love and obedience to the Lord. This is offered by people who walk in the Spirit and know the heart and revealed purposes of God. It is received by God as an acceptable sacrifice, pleasing to Him.

Strange fire is offered on the altar of our hearts when we presume to act without knowing the intent and will of God in a situation. Often it takes the form of doing good works instead of first seeking the Lord and finding His will and only then acting. It is rooted in the sin of presumption. Strange fire is offered by the carnally-minded person. And to be carnally-minded is death.

Useless fire is offered on the altar of our heart when we are merely going through the religious motions of serving God without the life of God being present. It is offered by the heart of one whose first love has grown cold. This is the offering of one backslidden in heart. You cannot be an effective Christian without the indwelling presence of Christ flowing unhindered in your life. God does not receive this kind of offering.

Fire speaks of worship unto the Lord. And God is seeking those who will worship Him in Spirit and Truth. Fire shines brightly in the darkness and can ignite a Christian's heart with the presence and glory of the Lord. He (the Lord) makes His ministers as flames of fire.

What kind of fire is burning of the altar of your heart today? What will you offer in sacrifice to the Lord?

A Grace of Thorns

While I'm not graced with a green thumb - it's more a dead brown kind of thumb - I do like occasionally working in my garden and puttering around my backyard. I dread trimming the flowers growing beside the house because every year, no matter how careful I am, I still manage to get pricked by thorns.

In almost every instance when thorns are mentioned in the Bible, it's in the context of judgment and curses. Thorns are mentioned as the bitter fruit of God cursing the earth in Genesis 3:18 — *"Thorns and thistles it shall bring forth to you."* The godless are unfavorably compared to thorns in 2 Samuel 23:6 — *"But godless men are all like thorns that are thrown away."* Hebrews 6:8 — *"If it bears thorns and thistles, it is worthless and near to being cursed; its end is to be burned."* The destiny of thorns is to be gathered together, thrown away, and burned.

Thorns represent the embodiment of the curse of sin. They are the antitheses of fruit, which is a picture of life and healing. Thorns are the barbed wire of fallen Creation. They serve as a sad testimony of the curse on fallen creation. Thorns often prick the unsuspecting causing pain and drawing a little blood. I believe this is to remind us that it is only by the shedding of blood is there remission for sin. His crown of thorns is a symbol of the great enemy of both God and man, the curse of Death.

While in Mexico, I stepped on the most hideous thorn bush imaginable. The thorns on this plant stuck out almost an inch and were it not for my pants, I would have been severely lacerated. The plant's name in Spanish translates to mean *Christ's thorns* in English. The mere thought of those piercing spikes going into my flesh made me recoil in horror.

We often contemplate the horrors of the Cross of Christ where our debts to God were paid off for us in full measure, but have you ever stopped to contemplate the meaning of the crown of thorns? The Cross is where God made the way to peace between himself and mankind. Colossians 1:20 — *"Making peace by the blood of His cross."* So, in the Plan of Redemption, what does the crown of thorns represent?

Matthew 27:29 — *"And plaiting a crown of thorns they put it on his head, and put a reed in his right hand. And kneeling before him they mocked him, saying, 'Hail, King of the Jews!'"* The thorns that were pressed together to form a crown estimated to have been anywhere from an inch long to as much as three inches. Talk about body piercing!

The first crown Jesus wore was a crown forged in mockery and shame. It was constructed of thorns which represent the curse of sin. According to Hebrews 12:2, *"Jesus ... who for the joy that was set before him endured the cross, despising the shame."* He willingly bore the Cross, and the crown of thorns, in joy. Was it painful? Horrifyingly so. Yet He considered your soul to be of greater worth than taking the very curse of Death on creation into His body.

Every anguished thought, all insanity, every tormenting thought and imagination that exalts itself against God, were all paid for in full as the curse was pierced through Christ's head. His innocent blood touched the very fruit of death - thorns to redeem us from anguish and tormenting thoughts.

Ironic that those who slammed those cursed spikes into His head will one day bow again at His feet and call Him **Lord of All.** And we who love His appearing will be able to stand before Him perfectly and fully forgiven and cast the crowns He gives us at his feet. He bore the crown of thorns so that we might one day wear a Crown of Life!

The Crown of Thorns was the payment made by God the Son Himself so that we might stand before Him as redeemed, regal sons and daughters wearing Crowns of Life! The thorns represented death, so that we might be crowned with Life. And who is the Life? None other than Jesus Himself!

Let the world mock you, speak scathingly of your faith, and hate you. Let them try to prick your heart with angry, hateful words. If they hated Him, they will hate you equally. And surely as He was raised from the dead unto everlasting life, so we shall be saved from death (the crown of thorns) unto eternal life by faith in the risen Son of God.

Consider this: sometimes those painful thorns in your life are God's secret Graces waiting to blossom unto life!

Holy Oil or Cheap Perfume?

Recently my wife bought a new perfume and tried it on without telling me. Husbands need heightened senses to things like new hairstyles, new dresses, the fact that the dishes are done, new perfumes, and so on. Mercifully, this was a sweet captivating concoction that made me merrily, willingly follow her around all day like a grinning puppy.

There's nothing like a really intoxicating perfume to further the noble cause of wife/husband bonding!

Once I was in a department store on a Sunday afternoon when a woman came sashaying her very Southern self by, swaying to a breeze only she could feel. You could smell her coming. She was wearing enough perfume to make a seeing-eye dog gag and run in terror. It was awful in a suffocating sense. My eyes watered while my defenseless sense of smell overdosed and died. I figured most women dab perfume on the way Catholics baptize - by a little sprinkle and some incomprehensible muttering. Well, this lady had to be a Protestant - she surely must have dipped herself all the way in!

As she passed me I actually gagged. My oxygen supply was momentarily cut off. I hoped she'd keep on moving or I feared she's pass out, too. Later, bees seemed to want to follow me home at a respectful distance. When I got home, I headed for the shower hoping we had some unscented soap.

There really is such a thing as too much of a good thing.

Perfume has been around since before the ancient Egyptians. Its original use was in arid lands where water was a premium and perfume served as deodorant for the hygienically challenged. God once commanded Moses to make a very special perfume - unlike anything else on earth -to be used as His holy anointing oil. This oil was made in Heaven.

Exodus 30: 31-35, 38 — *"This shall be my holy anointing oil throughout your generations. It shall not be poured upon the bodies of ordinary men, and you shall make no other like it in composition; it is holy, and it shall be holy to you. Whoever compounds any like it or whoever puts any of it on an outsider shall be cut off from his people."'* And the LORD said to Moses, *'Take sweet spices, stacte, and onycha, and galbanum, sweet spices with pure frankincense (of each shall there be an equal part), and make an incense blended as by the perfumer, seasoned with salt, pure and holy; Whoever makes any like it to use as perfume shall be cut off from his people.'"*

What is amazing about this oil is that it is a picture of the Holy Spirit. Ordinary men could not be anointed with this oil because God does not anoint flesh for His service. This perfume was to mark someone as holy and set apart unto the Lord.

I find verse 38 especially revealing. This anointing oil was not to be worn as perfume. Remember the woman in the store? Her perfume was worn to attract attention to herself. This anointing oil was to attract people to the beauty of the Lord.

The differences between the anointing oil and perfume are subtle but important. One leads men to you and the other is given with the intent to draw them to the Lord. Both of these ointments announce to all near that someone is coming but one draws men to you and the other points them to Christ. The anointing oil of God is *seasoned with salt*, which is a picture of a purifying, preservation agent. When salt looses its saltiness, it becomes useless. And when a man or woman of God rejects holiness, the anointing on their life loses its saltiness, too. The anointing becomes a cheap perfume that begins to stink.

Luke 4:18 — *"The Spirit of the Lord is upon me, because he has anointed me to preach good news to the poor. He has sent me to proclaim release to the captives and recovering of sight to the blind, to set at liberty those who are oppressed."* God warned His people that the anointing oil was not to be worn as a perfume or the wearer would be cut off from his people. The gifts of the Spirit are **not** given to further your own ends. The gifts and callings of God are without repentance but God will hold us accountable of how (and deep down in our hearts, why) we use His giftings.

When you stand ministering in the Lord's name, ask the Holy Spirit to search your heart. Musicians, are your songs a platform to build a great name for your-selves, or do they lead men to worship the Lord? Whatever your calling, do the gifts in your life lift up Jesus so that He may draw all men to Himself, or do they merely lift you up to be seen of men?

Are you wearing the holy anointing oil as the priest of God, or is it just cheap perfume?

The Knock-Off Anointing

There is a very special designer perfume made in by a chemical manufacturer in the USA. This perfume costs $5000 per half-once vial. It is incredibly expensive and extremely rare. There are only 2000 vials manufactured every year.

What makes this concoction so desirable is the way it interacts with a woman's pheromones. The chemicals in this perfume blend with her unique body chemistry to produce a fragrance unlike anyone else's. The perfume becomes uniquely hers.

You can go to any drugstore and find a similar perfume for $1.99 in a spray bottle. While this knock-off imitation is very close to the original, it is only an imitation. It smells the same on every woman who wears it. The sign on the perfume counter boast that is just like the real thing - but easily affordable. It's close, but it is still only a cheap imitation. There is nothing uniquely distinguishing to its scent. The plain truth is that it's still only toilet water.

The Bible has much to say in the area of anointing. Jesus began his public ministry by announcing the kind of anointing on his life. Luke 4:18 — *"The Spirit of the Lord is upon me, because he has anointed me to preach good news to the poor. He has sent me to proclaim release to the captives and recovering of sight to the blind, to set at liberty those who are oppressed."*

Jesus had an anointing that, like the designer perfume, was uniquely His. It was also incredibly expensive and extremely rare. Acts 10:38 — *"God anointed Jesus of Nazareth with the Holy Spirit and with power; how he went about doing good and healing all that were oppressed by the devil, for God was with him."*

The anointing Jesus had from the Father enabled Him to wage successful spiritual warfare and deliver people from sickness, disease, and captivity from the devil. Indeed, the anointing is given to break yokes of bondage. God said that when something is touched by the anointing oil, it is holy unto the Lord.

Exodus 30: 25, 31 — *"You shall make of these a sacred anointing oil blended as by the perfumer; a holy anointing oil it shall be."* *"And you shall say to the people of Israel, 'This shall be my holy anointing oil throughout your generations.'"*

God gave a curious command regarding this specially blended anointing oil.

Exodus 30: 32, 33 — *"It shall not be poured upon the bodies of ordinary men, and you shall make no other like it in composition; it is holy, and it shall be holy to you. Whoever compounds any like it or whoever puts any of it on an outsider shall be cut off from his people."*

The Lord commanded that His special blend of perfume (anointing oil) should never be imitated. He warned that He would cut off anyone who dared to make a cheap knock-off of it to use as perfume. This oil was a wonderful fragrance and the temptation would be to make a little *for personal use* and use it for *personal* perfume - and the anointing oil was to NEVER touch the flesh!

The church is full of knock-off anointing. The anointing given by God is unique to the life and vision of the individual that God has called to serve him. How many John Wimber wannabes are parading around imitating his unique ministry? Or Billy Graham, John Stott, Michael W. Smith, Joni Erickson Tada, Jack Hayford, or the pick someone you admire and insert their name here?

God has a unique anointing for the life of every believer that will consecrate him or her to the purposes of God. So many ministries are settling for a knock-off anointing, a cheap imitation of the real thing. The real anointing is incredibly expensive and extremely rare and it costs you your life to obtain it from God. So few are willing to pay the price to have a genuine anointing from God on their lives - so they settle for some cheap imitation brand name.

The cheap imitation brand names get on the *church market* when people begin to merchandise the anointing for profit and begin to raise up people like themselves instead of nurturing people who will simply follow Jesus.

We have lots of brand names today in the church market: Vineyard, Assembly of God, 1st Baptist, Nazarene, Campus Crusade for Christ, and so many more. The list seems endless, and God loves these people! God doesn't call us to find a comfortable ready made, mass produced anointing oil and then slap it on like after shave. He calls us to find Himself, and once we have sought for Him with all of our hearts, He himself will then anoint us for the unique ministry He has for us: unique, unlike any other.

Beloved, have you settled for a knock-off anointing, or have you paid the full price of consecration to have the real thing? Is that holy oil on you, or a cheap imitation knock-off of the real thing?

When Nations Tremble (A Prophetic Psalm)

When nations tremble it is because the Lord has roused Himself to walk among men. His approaching steps thunder like hoof beats from a stampeding herd of wild horses. He walks the lands searching hearts for righteousness. He hungers to taste the fruit of His Spirit growing sweetly among His tender vines. He longs to sip in communion with His saints the wine of His grace that He lavishes out freely. And for His enemies with each measured step He takes, kingdoms quake, countries fail, and nations tremble.

The Lord has measured the nations like grains of sand on righteous scales; the nations are less than nothing in His sight. While the kings of the earth plan their dark dread against God and His holy people, the Lord smiles sweetly at His covenant people even as He laughs His terrifying laugh at the wicked. He shall suddenly rise and rage against them and in a burning moment, they shall be no more. The terrifying echo of His laugh shall haunt them forever.

God is sifting the nations even as grain is sifted. He is tossing up and down, back and forth, shaking all that can be shaken. He lets tyrants and evil men rise up to the measure of their own sin, and He hurls them back scorned to be forgot-ten in the dust. Pharaohs have risen and vanished, Kings have reigned by the score, Presidents and Prime Ministers etch their competitive mark in the fading wind and they all finally wither away. The man who fears the Lord remains steadfast forever.

When nations tremble they learn the fear of the Lord. He has roused Himself to walk among men. He is coming with His reward for those who love His coming. For those who oppose Him, He will meet in battle and subdue them. Devils will fall, chains shall be shattered, the earth will seem as a scorched field, and God alone will be glorified in that great and terrible day. As that day is quickly approaching, the shadow of its dread falls like a curtain across the lands, and the nations tremble.

Pharaoh's Magicians

I have been distressed for some time at the spiritual state of the world, especially the USA. You cannot look at any form of mass media without being inundated with Psychics and their claims. Master psychics, 10 free minutes of readings, horoscopes, lucky numbers...it's all witchcraft. I began to feel helpless against this onslaught.

I woke up around 3:30 a.m. one morning and the Lord directed me to the Bible story of the confrontation of Moses and Aaron, representing the Lord, with Pharaoh and his magicians, representing Satan. God began to show me that Satan was in fact NOT winning and the Lord is indeed in control. This present rise of false, wicked spirituality will actually set the stage for God to display His power, mercy, and judgments to the world before He returns.

In Exodus 7, Aaron threw down his rod before Pharaoh and his court at the Lord's command, and it became a serpent. Pharaoh called in his wise men, sorcerers and magicians (EX 7:11) and each duplicated Aaron's feat by their *secret arts*. Then Aaron's staff swallowed up their staffs! God began to demonstrate to these idolaters who really was Lord of the universe.

Later in Exodus 7:20-22 Aaron stretched his rod over the Nile and the waters turned to blood. The magicians could duplicate this by their *secret arts* too.

Over in Exodus 8:6-7, Aaron stretched out his rod and called forth frogs. The pharaoh's magicians were able to copy this, too. This was beginning to look like a Mexican stand off between Moses and Aaron and Pharaohs magicians.

Ever heard the expression, *"Give a fool enough rope and eventually he'll hang himself?"* That's just what happened! In Exodus 8: 16-16, Aaron called for a plague of gnats. Pharaoh's magicians could NOT duplicate this and, give them credit, they really tried. These magicians began to get a real revelation. *"This is the finger of God,"* they said to Pharaoh - whom they worshiped as a god. This was probably not something that a false messiah would care to hear from his priests. God's enemies began to testify of His greatness. What does the New Testament say about every knee bowing and every tongue confessing WHO is Lord?

Finally in Exodus 9: 8-11, after Moses threw soot into the air the and festering boils broken out on men and animals, *the magicians could not stand before Moses*! It was significant that Moses did this miracle and not Aaron. Aaron represents the covenant people of God - but the Lord made Moses as GOD to Pharaoh. By allegory, it was God himself showing the magicians to be frauds!

So what does this have to do with the psychic craze sweeping the world? The Lord told Pharaoh that it was in fact He who raised him (Pharaoh) up to demonstrate His power to the world. Pharaoh's magicians who withstood Aaron and Moses were shown finally to be spiritually bankrupt frauds even as they testified to God's greatness.

For a time, the Lord is allowing psychics to rise up and declare things by their *secret arts* and they can mimic, to a point, the gifts of the Holy Spirit. The day is quickly coming when the psychics will not be able to duplicate the signs and wonders that God will do and they will finally fall before the Lord, *not being able to stand before Him* and declare *"This is the finger of God!"* Powerless, they will point the world to Jesus who is LORD! All those who followed their lies will then be given opportunity to repent and "call upon the name of the Lord and be saved!"

Talk about saving $3.99 a minute.

Don't be dismayed at the apparent march of evil. Don't sweat the psychics. Psalm 2:4 says the Lord *laughs* at the wicked because He sees their end. He will arise and be with His church as a dread champion. God will silence the magicians of our time and He alone will be glorified!

A Dead Person's Corsage

There are defining moments in life when desperate times call for stupid measures.

My wife and I once lived across the street from a cemetery. Our neighbors never bothered us much except when it got windy. We had a no turnover, stable neighborhood, at least across the street. It was not uncommon for wreaths, ribbons, and things to blow into our yard. One morning I walked out to find a R.I.P. wreath snagged nearly perfectly centered on my car grill. I prayed before driving to work in case it was an omen!

When we first moved into our home we had a dumb young married people's argument - the subject now forgotten. Things were stressful and heated and I was momentarily blinded to common sense. How do you heal a broken heart? I went outside to cool off and took a short walk with my son.

I needed flowers.

O.K., throw your stones; judge me as sick, sick, sick but I was DESPERATE. It was dusk and I was feeling stupid for losing my temper and was trying to concoct a way to apologize to my wife. That's when I noticed the discarded mound of flowers, ribbons, and wreaths at the back of the cemetery. Inspiration hit.

If you're not a young husband, you couldn't possibly understand but I had to do something. No, I didn't rob anyone's grave (I have scruples) but I walked over to the trash mound and helped myself to a single discarded flower. My plan was simple and elegant. Get the flower, take it home as a peace offering, and all would be well again. I would go to the florist in the morning and replace it with a dozen more flowers and no one would be the wiser.

I walked in and fumbled an apology to my wife and had my son hand her the flower. That's when, too late, I noticed the flower was silk.

I had just given my wife a dead person's corsage. As I said, sometimes desperate times call for stupid measures.

After the shock subsided and she quit laughing, we worked through the disagreement. I never did buy the replacement flower hoping to let the incident pass forgotten and unnoticed in our personal married history.

While my neighbors rest in peace, I can rest assured that my wife will *never* let me forget this one. Such is the painful price of foolishness.

Sometimes we find ourselves pressured of circumstances to simply act - without thinking or seeking God. The Lord knows the end from the beginning and He promises that if we need wisdom, ASK and He'll freely give it to us. Most people fail here because they don't wait for the answer when they do remember to ask. Don't make seeking God your last resort. Seek Him first in all things. It can save you wasted time, pain, and embarrassment. Don't allow pressure to bully you into acting without God's guidance and wisdom.

If life hands you a flower in your darkest hour, make sure it isn't silk before passing it on!

The Chicken Gun

There is an unconfirmed rumor that NASA has done it again! First, they put a man on the moon. Now they've apparently developed a chicken gun. Yep, a high velocity projectile poultry cannon used to test the impact of birds on fast moving aircraft.

Ain't science grand?

This device is designed to scientifically measure the impact of birds hitting aircraft windshields and other sensitive areas. I don't imagine these birds are volunteers since they go screaming from Zero to 10+ Gs in a matter of seconds only to splat into their targets at better than 500 miles-per-hour. I imagine that the last thing to go through the poor bird's are their feet. Fortunately, the scientists at NASA decided early on to use only dead birds lest they run afoul of the law.

Where this gets especially funny is that the British Air Force allegedly purchased one of NASA's chicken guns to experiment with on their own planes. They placed the corpse of the deceased chicken into the gun, aimed it at an RAF plane, and fired. This chicken proved mightier than a cannon ball! Instead of splatting into the windshield, it burst right through splintering the glass, shattering the control counsel and mashing up the cockpit.

Three times the stunned Brits fired NASA's chicken gun at their multi-million pound plane and three times the results were disastrous. Finally, they e-mailed NASA for clarifications of the instructions. NASA replied with these three words:

"Thaw the chicken."

Laugh at the frozen chicken cannonball but people really aren't all that different. God calls us to cultivate a soft heart towards Him and others. Hebrews 4:7 — *"Today, when you hear his voice, do not harden your hearts."* A thawed chicken corpse splats pretty easily at 500 miles per hour but a frozen one becomes a functional weapon that can take out a sophisticated, hi-tech fighter plane.

A hard heart is a weapon of satan. Paul wrote in Romans 2:5 — *"By your hard and impenitent heart you are storing up wrath for yourself on the day of wrath when God's righteous judgment will be revealed."* Even Job had a revelation of the origin of hardness of heart. Speaking of Leviathan, in Job 41:24, he exclaimed, *"His heart is hard as a stone, hard as the nether millstone."* He went on to call this creature the king of the sons of pride.

Hardness of heart is a symptom of the real disease: pride!

Men harden their hearts when they won't heed the gentle voice of the Spirit of God. And the more they rebel and insist on going their own way the harder their hearts become. Like the frozen chicken, we can inadvertently become a weapon in the hands of the devil when we grow icy and hard inside.

In the natural body, a heart hardens when the arteries clog up with poison and finally kill off the body. It's pretty similar in the spirit with the hidden man of the heart. When you begin to grow hard, the poison of pride does its deadly work, and you begin to get weak spiritually. Eventually, its venom kills you.

If you've gone hard inside, perhaps by an offense, or a failure, or by just neglecting your walk with God, cry out to Him to soften you up inside again. Allow the Holy Spirit to massage His healing oil into your wounded heart and drive the hardness away.

Just like the chicken in NASA's poultry gun, when you die you're gonna be suddenly propelled towards the heavens like a missile. I can't help but think that those with soft, gentle hearts will land smoothly at the Pearly gates. I suspect those with hard hearts will ricochet right off of the Gate, to another destination!

Learn a lesson from the chickens who have gone before you: **Thaw Your Heart!**

The Mexican Woman's Leg

The Lord has delivered me of a lifelong obsessive fear of heights. Before this mighty deliverance occurred, an incident occurred which illustrates the verse Psalms 34:4 — *"I sought the LORD, and he answered me, and delivered me from all my fears."* I add that Goliath of Gath was a mere 10 feet tall. The Arch is almost 700 feet tall. It stands as a giant among giants!

My beautiful son David fell in love with the St. Louis Arch. Ever see a picture of that big upside down aluminum horseshoe overlooking the Mississippi? That's the one. It serves as a constant reminder to me that engineers have a basically warped sense of humor. Anyway, when David was three years old he asked me to take him to the top.

Yeah, right.

I don't know if it was his persistence or my fear of looking like a scardy cat, but somehow I agreed to take him to the top for his 5th birthday. A moment later, two years had zoomed past.

"Daddy?"

Yes, son of my love.

"It's time for the ride to the very top of the Arch. (Dramatic pause). *You did promise, didn't you, Daddy? And you NEVER break a promise."*

That Shirley Temple smile of his is arresting. Those trusting eyes had me. The indignity of it all was that I had to PAY for the privilege of the sheer terror of getting in that metal monstrosity. As we went through the lines like prisoners hoping for a final smoke and blindfold, I tried to remain calm. I sort of comboed whistling and praying in tongues while in line, trying real hard not to sweat.

When got to the elevators, there were these 6 seats inside like those pods from *Invasion of the Bodysnatchers*, when that grinning snot of an escort invited us to *"relax, and enjoy the ride."* He kind of looked at me for a moment grinned real big, and said, *"Relax, sir. We haven't lost one. Yet."*

Slam! The escape hatch shut and there we all were - trapped like elves at the North Pole. Rumor has it they never get out alive, either.

My son rode on the next car with my brother David who engineered the whole thing and I later found out, had *reminded* his nephew of daddy's promise. I rode with my wife, a Mexican couple and their kids whom we didn't know. I grabbed the rail next to me and held on tight. I was panting, doing breathing exercises in a vain attempt to remain calm. I could feel gravity screaming for me not to leave but the cables were too strong. Up, up, ohmygosh, UP in that tiny coffin-sized cabin to the top.

They say it only sways 19 inches in the wind. Big deal. All that means it that if you time it just right, you can hurl an extra two feet should you get sick at the top.

When we finally stopped at the top, I breathed a sigh of relief. I hadn't messed my drawers or thrown up. I had kept my promise, however grudgingly, to my son. All I had to do was not look out the window and I would be fine. That's when I became aware everyone in the cabin was laughing.

I slowly peeled my eyes open, unsquinting a bit and the first thing I saw was the lovely Mexican woman next to me with a shocked, bemused look on her face. She was laughing. Hard. Her husband was laughing; their kids were laughing. My wife was snorting and snotting till she nearly choked with glee.

That's when I noticed the *rail* I was white knuckling was in fact that poor Mexican woman's leg!

Not feeling a need to apologize, I politely thanked her for the company and got out of the cabin with my dignity intact. I walked to the window to keep from DYING of embarrassment. That's when I finally got sick.

Fear is a foolish thing. I was worked up over what amounted to nothing. I don't sit next to Mexican women any more, either. Call it a precaution on my part. Now my wife knows instinctively to hold my hand. And I will never ride up the Arch again! Not out of fear. I finally figured out that some attractions are best left for the tourists.

Domesticating Jesus

I went to visit a newly married friend of mine who had just returned from a belated honeymoon in the mountains. He couldn't wait to show me his new kitty. I leaned over the towel-filled box and gently stroked the curled up sleeping kitty who had a marvelous coat that felt closer to leather than cat fur. And from somewhere beneath the towels kitty suddenly let out savage roar.

No, it wasn't a gently meow, but a guttural, low, menacing, fierce, hunter killing-the-prey sort of roar. And kitty suddenly peered up at me with the greener than green eyes, deftly swiping at my outstretched hand with razor sharp claws. I jumped back with a sudden revelation: kitty wasn't a kitty at all. She was a ferocious bobcat.

My golden-hearted, if sometimes dull-witted, friend explained that they found her wandering along side a road. *"In the mountains?"* I surmised. Yes, in the mountains. It was raining and kitty needed a home so they good-heartedly wrapped her up in a sweater and brought her all the way to Missouri.

He got kinda quiet for a moment responding to the look of disbelief in my eyes and said, *"She's not a cat, is she?"* I quietly suggested we immediately take *kitty* to an animal reserve before neighborhood dogs and small children started to disappear.

You can put a bell and collar on a bobcat; you can give her canned fish, stroke her fur and buy her all the catnip she can handle. When she is hungry, she will hunt and kill because that is her nature. She is an untamed creature and no matter how well your intentions, you cannot domesticate a wild animal.

Consider the God of all creation. Try as we might, as good as our religious intentions are, we cannot domesticate him. He is not a house pet or a genie in a bottle to respond to our tricks or treats. He is still the Ancient of Days, still God Almighty.

Men invent doctrines that allegedly force Him to perform in response to certain phrases and rituals. Others attempt to steal away truths about His nature and goodness and recreate Him according to their own desires, while others vainly dismiss Him as a by-product of evolution. No matter how you may try to declaw Him, make Him exclusive to your particular little group, or chain Him to a *what God used to do* worldview, He is still the Lord of Creation. He roars in Malachi 3:6 — *"For I am the LORD, I change not!"*

To domesticate an animal takes generations of selectively breeding certain traits in and out of animal lines. You cannot do this with God because before all of eternity was, He existed. He is simply, exclusively, uniquely I AM. Perhaps, like Job, the Lord will answer humanity out of a whirlwind and ask of us who darkens His counsel without knowledge. May we have the wisdom to finally shut up before Him.

Instead of debating over ways to domesticate and manipulate the God of all creation, perhaps if we would humble ourselves before Him and look upon the splendor of His light and be utterly enraptured with the beauty of His holiness, we might then declare with the angels the unchanging truth about the King of Kings.

Revelation 11:17 — *"We give you thanks, O Lord God Almighty, who is, who was, and who is to come; because you have taken to yourself great power, and you alone reign."*

Concerning the Lion of the tribe of Judah, the Bible declares, in Joel 3:16 — *"The LORD also shall roar out of Zion, and utter his voice from Jerusalem; and the heavens and the earth shall shake."*

The Great I AM simply is, and cannot be tamed.

In The Shadow of Babel

Genesis 11: 3-4 — "*And the whole earth was of one language and expression... And they said, 'Come, let us build us a city and a tower whose top reaches into the heavens'... And the Lord came down to see the city and the tower...And the Lord said ... 'Come, let Us go down there and confuse their language'... So the Lord scattered them abroad from that place upon the face of the whole earth, and they gave up building the city.*"

This is the story of the building of the infamous tower of Babel. Remember that in the original plan for man in Genesis 1: 28, God commanded men to "*be fruitful, multiply, and fill the earth.*" It was His desire for us to fill the earth with people who were little reflections of Himself. After sin entered the world, men began to live closely together in defiance of the command to go forth.

Look carefully at the wording of this passage. Men decided that they were going to build a tower that reached up into the heavens, the abode of God. They worked and sweated in a rebellious attempt to somehow reach God by their own efforts. Has anything under the sun ever really changed?

God came down to look at their work and knew it would fail. In His mercy, He scattered their languages so that they could not understand each other. There was incredible confusion. People began to have to search for others whose language they could understand and then group with them. These like groups began to migrate together away from Babylon and so begin to finally fulfill God's command to go into all of the world.

This event foreshadowed of the mystery of God's plan of salvation. God knew men couldn't reach Him by their efforts to work their way up, so He had to come down to them. Men foolishly strive to meet God *in the heavens* as an equal. He finally *came down* in the form of the man Christ Jesus to meet us on our level to save us from our sins so that we could really meet with God in heaven - as part of the adoring creation worshipping our lovely Creator.

Babylon was the first attempt at a demonic scheme to create a one-world government. There was a universal culture, a universal language, and an attempt to somehow raise ourselves up as gods *in the heavens*. Sound familiar?

The world today is much in the same mode as it was in the days of Genesis. We are again under the shadow of Babel. There is a marked push to unify mankind. Through mass media, a one-world culture based on shallow American values is emerging. We have the United Nations, a one-world police force that is gaining power. We have one universal language that the world uses to transact business and government, English. All that is really needed now is for a One world leader to finally emerge and declare Himself to be (and I suspect declare the people of the earth to be as a corporate) God.

I am drawing two profound truths from this story. The first is that, like the people of the plain of Shinar, humanity is on a collision course with God. The second sad truth is for the church.

Many errant preachers today attempt to deify the born again man to the level of godhood. They quote Jesus who in John 10:34 said, *"Ye are gods."* What they miss is the origin of this quote. Jesus was quoting from Psalm 82: 6-7. It states, *"Ye are gods...but you shall die as men."* God was mocking these people in their self-inflated deity. He was telling them that they were not Gods. Asaph ends this Psalm with this prayer, *"Arise, O God, judge the earth! For to you alone belong the nations."*

God does not have little gods walking the earth. If you

search the origin of the desire to be as god, it was birthed in the dark, blinded pride of Satan's heart when he said, "*I will ascend...I will be like the Most High.*" If godhood is your goal, you'll keep satan and his minions company throughout eternity along with all of the other would-be *gods* who will be finally cast from the presence of the Lord into the Lake of Fire.

If you are sitting under any teacher who is teaching that you are a god, run for your very life. Get out of that ministry, shake the dust from your feet, and denounce the apostasy you have been supporting. You're being set up to buy into the End Time deception which according to Matthew 24:24 will "*deceive, if possible, the very elect.*" Men are only men. God alone is God. His word says, "*If there are gods formed after me, I do not know about it.*"

The second truth is for the church. God moves by His Spirit and begins to revive his people. Sinners start calling upon the Lord's name. We then entomb revival by gathering the people of God together and stamp our name on it. We quit being salt and light as we withdraw into a Christian subculture. Like the people of Shinar, we quit going into all of the world and begin to build our own version of God's city.

I believe there is a street based revival coming that will confuse the religious institutions of man even as God confused the people at Babel. In Matthew 24:14, We are commanded to "*preach this Gospel to every nation, and then the end shall come.*" God is going to birth a missionary zeal for the nations into his people to finish the harvest of souls before He comes. Yes, there will be administration and organization. Yes, there will be human leadership. It was God Himself who placed apostles, prophets, evangelists, pastors and teachers into the Body. But all of this will be under the Leading of the Spirit under the Lordship of the head of the church, the Lord Jesus Christ.

God will expose the petty self-serving kingdoms men have built with His sacred blood for the scams they are. I believe, like the people of Shinar, we will *give up building the city*, and begin to seek a city *whose builder and maker is God*. Then God will come down in the person of His Son to judge the earth. The world today is rebuilding the tower of Babel on a global scale. Learn the lessons of Babel and don't be caught as one unaware.

Turk or Porky?

When my little brother was a lowly private in the army, he was once meandering his way through a chow line. The military serves a pressed meat concoction that is either turkey or pork; you really can't tell the difference between them by mere sight. Military culinary critics claim that, when soaked with gravy, you can't taste the difference, either.

This pressed meat concoction is jadedly referred to in morbid undertones as *"the other white meat."* Some suspect pressed meat to be an extended part of the military's *"Don't Ask, Don't Tell"* policy.

Sometimes, for no apparent reason, things will strike you as gut-wrenchingly hilarious when no one else is laughing. And the harder you try to explain the absurdity that is reducing you to chuckles and tears to a bemused onlooker, the more you laugh, especially when they just don't get it. It's a vicious circle.

My baby brother was going through a chow line with a burly Sergeant following behind him. When he got to the white meat, his tongue kind of twisted as he pointed to *"the other white meat"* and asked the cook, *"Is that turk or porky?"*

He started to giggle, quickly recaptured his military composure, and tried to rephrase the question. *"I mean, is that turk or porky?"* And he started peeling with laughter. The Sergeant behind him eventually threw him out of the chow line for causing a disturbance. He nearly crawled out the door gasping for breath - the more he tried to stop , the harder he laughed.

He never did find out if it was turkey or pork on the menu. They wouldn't let him have chow that night, either.

He was laughing too hard to care.

Sometimes it's hard to distinguish one thing from another

because they look so similar. My brother couldn't discern between the *white meats* of turkey and pork. They looked so much alike that you needed to take a bite to figure out what the *white meat* of the meal was.

1 John 2:15 — *"Do not love the world or the things in the world. If any one loves the world, love for the Father is not in him."*

When God calls us, He infuses us with His Spirit, and sets us against the flow and current of this present world system. We become citizens of Heaven, heralds of the new coming order of the reign of Jesus Christ. This world is no longer our hope or home and we become as strangers and aliens on the earth.

The saint becomes as a city set on a hill whose light can be seen. We begin to take on holy character and to exhibit the life of Christ. Kingdoms begin to clash in conflict as we begin to make godly choices that set us against the old world system. Many believers begin to weary in doing well and start to faint. There is a great temptation to begin to compromise and go along with the world on what are first deemed unessentials.

As this trend accelerates, the presence of the Lord begins to wane in our lives. We go from white hot to lukewarm - while being congratulated by those who have backslidden before us on our new found *maturity*. We begin to lose the flavor of heaven and begin to look, live, and talk like the world.

James 4:4 — *"Do you not know that friendship with the world is enmity with God? Therefore whoever wishes to be a friend of the world makes himself an enemy of God."*

Being a disciple of Jesus Christ has an unchanging price. Luke 9:23 — *"And he said to all, 'If any man would come after me, let him deny himself and take up his cross daily and follow me.'"* We have to daily decide to deny ourselves, pick up his cross, and follow Him. There is no other way to faithfully serve God.

When the world comes to *"taste and see that the Lord is good"* by taking a bite out of your flesh, what will they taste? Will they find the sweet peace and character of Jesus or the anger and rage of the fallen world?

What will they taste: turk or porky?

Haunted Souls

There was an abandoned house not far from where I grew up that was rumored to be haunted by the ghost of its deceased owner. The place moaned eerily, almost forlornly in the rural Iowa wind. It sat on a small hill just outside of town looking always ghostly and uninviting in the moon-light.

People sped past it just a bit when driving - and the narrowed road wasn't the reason. The house always evoked memories of past emotions rather than a specific past event. If for no other reason than that, I would say the house was haunted.

Have you ever walked down a street and looked intently into a stranger's eye? I've met people who were chained to some event in the past, a sad, beguiled prisoner of time and circumstance. Somewhere, sometime there was a war waged deep in their soul and they lost the fight, and became a prisoner of war to their own past. A wounding chained them to a darkness they feel condemned to repeat; from whose poisoned clutches they are powerless to escape.

Souls can be haunted, too.

What haunts you in the recesses of your soul? Is it some forgotten love, a dream decayed, turned to ashes and dust? A voice echoing from the dim past calling out to you reverberating with cries and sorrows only you can hear? Is there a haunted look that suddenly flashes through your eyes that instantly transports you from the present to a tortured time from long ago?

Our bodies are called temples of the Holy Spirit. We were made with a place inside of us that is set apart as the dwelling place of God's Spirit. When something else begins to usurp that sovereign place of communion with God, we become haunted souls. There is some other spirit beginning to rule and reign over us that is not the Spirit of Christ.

When someone becomes mortally wounded in the essence of who and what they are, they begin to close up, harden inside, and the wound begins to fester. Somewhere something begins to go sour and instead of living each new day that bursts joyously with the overflowing mercies of God, they begin to live that dread-ed old day over and over again. They go out of sync with the new day and get lost in a merciless maze in a frozen, dark unchangeable past that terrorizes them.

Jesus came to set prisoners free. You don't need to be under the thumb of a military tyrant to be a prisoner. Sometimes the heartbreaking past is enough of a dreaded master to make you a captive soul in need of liberation and freedom. Healing doesn't always come overnight in a single prayer. Deliverance often comes by minute degree and decrees of God's promises - but healing will come as we begin to take every haunting thought captive to the obedience of Christ.

If you're haunted by some specter from the past, Jesus came to seek and save that which was lost. God's will is to restore you to wholeness, and make all things new. Let the haunting end by surrendering your *prisoner status* to your Liberator.

Ask Him to break the chains of shame that hold you in needless bondage. If the past haunts you, prowling and stalking like a ravaging monster in the ruins of your mind, call out to God from the deep recesses of your shattered heart. A broken and contrite heart he never rejects. Give your haunted past a funeral service and lay your ghosts to rest by burying them in the healing blood of the Lamb.

He came to set prisoners free. Souls were made to be free, and were not intended to be playgrounds for marauding ghosts that should have been buried long ago.

The Warrior is a Rat

Behold, the lowly rat. The only thing lower than a rat on the descending social scale is a dead rat. Blamed for everything from the Black Plague that killed half of Europe to eating 20% of India's annual grain produce (while being worshiped as a god no less!), the rat stands as an enduring symbol of notoriety.

We've had dirty rats, ratfinks, the rat race, snitches who rat out their friends, even rats who abandon sinking ships. In New York City we've had Donuts a la rat, stinking rats, and surely the only good rat is a dead rat. Go on, tell your kids to be brave as lions, be as cunning as a shark, and even be as industrious as the lowly, squishable ant. So who ever tells little impressionable Johnny to be *anything* using the rat as a favorable role model?

Did you know that rats, dead rats specifically, helped win the Second World War against Nazi Germany? The comparisons between Hitler's goose-stepping soldiers and sneaky vermin are not lost on anyone today save a few rat-eyed racists who just don't get it that Hitler and his pack of two-legged brown-shirted vermin were, alas, not the good guys.

Ahhh, those intrepid English, what didn't they try in attempt to stop the Nazis. One of their wartime operatives in Special Operations Executive (SOE) dreamed up a poetic way to fight the Germans in occupied Europe: use exploding dead rats.

Recently released papers from the SOE concerning the clandestine activities revealed plans designed to hurt the German war effort. One idea was to stuff the carcasses of dead rats with explosives and stash them near power plant generators in the hopes that workmen would throw the disease carrying stiffs into the fire for immediate cremation. Hopefully, the patriotic rodents would then give their all as they blew the power plants to kingdom come.

Who could have ever imagined that a dynamite suppository

given to dead rats would prove an effective cure for Nazism? It was certainly a more patriotic end for the rat than to end up as an alley cat snack.

The exploding rat carcass plot was uncovered early on by the Germans so only 100 of the explosive vermin were ever actually produced. The discovery, as it turned out, was even more effective than the plot. Fearful Germans began hunting for rat corpses in earnest. Their fears overrode their national morale as they scrambled to find, and eliminate, any dead rats they could find. The hunt for dead incendiary rodents gave the Germans absolute fits and kept them from focusing on their war effort.

Can't you just see the unflappable Sir Winston Churchill at his desk privately snickering, chuckling himself to tears every time he thought of explosive rats giving their all for Queen and country? The lowly rat proved a modern plague to the infestation of Aryan vermin in a certain Berlin bunker, all for the glory of the Allies.

The devil uses these sort of distraction tactics to keep Christians from being about their Father's business, too. Ever find an exploding rat in the form of hearing negative gossip about yourself? How about having to defend yourself against false accusations? Perhaps the most effective exploding rat scenario is worry about the future. What if this, what if that - while present day life slips by you into the cracks of time lost forever.

Just as there were only a few of the dynamite laden rodents ever produced, so only a few of your worst fears will ever come true. And when they do, what could you have done to stop them from manifesting? Probably very little.

There is a war on. Don't allow fear to magnify the enemy's power so that he appears greater than God. See the distractions for the military diversion tactics they are. Don't allow your fear of exploding dead rats to keep you from giving your all for God today.

A Place of Separation

Exodus 8: 20-23 — *"Say to him (Pharaoh), Thus says the LORD, 'Let my people go, that they may serve me. If you will not let my people go, behold, I will send swarms of flies on you. But on that day I will set apart the land of Goshen, where my people dwell, so that no swarms of flies shall be there; that you may know that I am the LORD in the midst of the earth.'"*

Exodus 9: 23-26 — *"Then Moses stretched forth his rod toward heaven; and the LORD sent thunder and hail, and fire... Only in the land of Goshen, where the people of Israel were, there was no hail."*

Exodus 10:21-23 — *"Then the LORD said to Moses, 'Stretch out your hand toward heaven that there may be darkness over the land of Egypt, a darkness to be felt'... but all the people of Israel had light where they dwelt."*

Goshen was a special place in Egypt where God's chosen people lived. It rep-resents a place of separation from the world system. It was a place of refuge for God's people who lived in Egypt (the world) but were not of the world. Goshen was a kind of refuge for God's people. As Israel's children began to multiply, the Egyptians began to enslave them and use them for forced labor.

There is something about living a separated life that is really given to Christ that makes you the target of unpopularity and occasional mockery. I know a dear sister in the Lord who is rumored to be gay by her co-workers because she refuses to date or participate the sexual side of office politics. She is wait-ing for the man God has for her. Righteousness has a price. She is patient, trusting in God, knowing that His chosen man will be perfect for her.

When the judgments of God began to fall on Egypt and her

idols, the people living in Goshen were kept safe. When Moses called forth a darkness so thick you could feel it, there was LIGHT in Goshen. God's people were spared many of the judgments. Why? Because they were living in a place of separation, a place of consecration unto God.

Does separation mean retreating from the world? No! How else could we be salt and light? Separation is a heart issue. It is an internal standard that says regardless of what goes on around me, I choose to honor God in all things. Separation means we love the sinners without partaking in the sin. Separation means we go heart-first into the world with the Good News about Jesus but we do not live as if we were a part of its corruption. Separation is living consciously under the all seeing eyes of God.

A non-Christian friend, faced with a difficult problem, called me and asked for prayer. This person hasn't been open to any of my talk about Jesus. I was surprised by his request for prayer and asked him why he wanted prayer. He replied, *"Because I know you know God. He's the only one who can help me with this."* Perhaps they're listening more than we realize. And he did later come to faith in Christ.

God makes a real distinction between His people and people of the world who reject him. Living a separate life will mark you but will protect you, too. For instance, if you don't want sexually transmitted diseases, don't commit the sin. Living in purity will protect you from the horrifying sexually transmitted plagues that are even now sweeping the earth.

Holiness is a real refuge for God's people.

In the verses quoted above, flies are a symbol of demons in scripture. Satan is called the Lord of the flies. God put a protective hedge around His people and wouldn't let the devils feast on those who were called by His name. In the Last Days when men's hearts are failing from fear, the people of God will walk securely trusting and resting in God. One day we shall sit in judgment of these fallen angels.

When thunder, hail and fire fell (speaking of divine judgments from Heaven), God's people were not affected, because we were already judged at Calvary! Our sins were taken away. I am convinced that if God's people had left the land of Goshen, they would have perished in the same judgments. By living in a place of separation from the world, they were kept safe.

2 Corinthians 6:17 — *"Therefore come out from them, and be separate from them, says the Lord, and touch nothing unclean; then I will welcome you."*

It is when we yield ourselves fully to Jesus and say, *"Lord, not my will but yours,"* that we become a really useful person in this present world. If we live by the standards (in the power of His indwelling Holy Spirit) of the world to come, we ironically become useful vessels in this lifetime of deliverance for those who are perishing without Christ.

The Egyptians were crying out to their gods when the judgments fell. Yet there was no deliverance because Psalms 4:3 says, *"But know that the LORD has set apart the godly for himself; the LORD hears when I call to him."* God hears the prayers of the righteous.

So is there a price to pay for living holy in an ungodly world? 2 Timothy 3:12 — *"Indeed all who desire to live a godly life in Christ Jesus will be persecuted."* That kind of persecution is a promise in the Word of God. You become set against the ebb and flow of the world and people think you're crazy. But there is an even greater price for not living a separated life. Ask Lot's wife.

As God is judging this world, as economic turmoil sweeps

through country after country who have worshiped mammon, as hurricanes wash away city after city, as sexual disease plagues continue to kill, as all of the idols of Egypt are judged and shown to be barren and powerless to save, God will protect His people - indeed He will prosper and bless - those who will live in a place of separation. The fear of the Lord is the beginning of wisdom, and that wisdom will keep you safe when there is no safe place to flee.

2 Peter 2:9 — *"The Lord knows how to rescue the godly from trial, and to keep the unrighteous under punishment until the day of judgment."*

In the story of the judgments on Egypt, the greater story was the final deliverance of God's people into the Promised Land. One day our Lord Himself shall return with a shout and we shall ever be with Him! Until that day, live a life of separation from sin that is pleasing to the Lord.

I saw a commercial that extolled the virtues of using *protection* during sexual immorality because it would minimize your chances of getting STDs. Why not stop these horrible plagues at their source? Obey God and don't participate in the sin, and you will walk in perfect *protection*. Holiness will keep you alive and well while others, like in Revelation 16:11 — *"Blasphemed the God of heaven because of their pains and their sores, and repented not of their deeds."*

From Prisoner 354-B9

DISCLAIMER: I was praying in the Spirit about 3 am when this came. I was wide-awake yet had a very real dream. One minute I was walking and praying, the next I was standing in a prison cell in the former Soviet Union facing this prisoner; and then I was back again. What I received I pass on for prayer and reflection.

To My American cousins in Christ,

It's frigidly cold here this morning. My cell is unheated and I cannot feel my legs. This is a blessing. Today I will be beaten and tortured before breakfast and I will not feel the pain as much. Numbness from the cold makes the tortures bear-able. I will have to remember to scream on cue so as not to upset the guards. I wonder if they are as bored with my cries as I am with their beatings. In prison, everything becomes routine, even torture.

I prayed for you again. I have much time on my hands here and thankfully no blood. I once heard a rumor that the churches in America each had a complete Bible of their very own. Could such a thing be true? Once at a house church meeting, just before my last arrest - how many years has it been - I actually held a page of Scripture in my own hands and was allowed to read it to the church. I myself was holding the Word of God. I knew then that I was favored of the Lord. Such a great honor.

In my dream today I went to Heaven again and one of the Splendid Ones spoke with me about you. He showed me the great Russian bear - not at all dead as you have supposed - hibernating, rejuvenating, readying to attack you. Her sharp paws were unsheathed ready to slice and maul you into submission. *"Why do they disarm?"* I asked, and the Splendid One replied, *"They are at ease in Zion but soon will be at ease no more."*

"I do not understand," I replied a bit confused.

"Many saints of the West have become wealthy and do not know that they are really wretched and poor and miserable and blind and naked. They usually equate the blessing of God with having money. They do not know of His true riches," said the glorious being.

Then Jesus Himself entered the place where we were talking. All bowed low and worshiped but I wept bitterly. Though He knew the answer, he asked me why I wept so. "Lord," I said, "Your sufferings only lasted a few days and mine have gone on for years. I have suffered much more than you. Why?"

With a great compassion, He seemed to look right through me (I felt him do this). He said, "Son, I have allowed you to sip suffering in small swallows so that your faith would not fail. I swallowed the dregs of the poison of sin whole. It was a torture you could never understand and it would have undone you. You have drank of my cup. Be patient a while longer."

I begged His forgiveness. His hand raised only to wipe my tears away and He held me close in understanding. I breathed in the perfume of His grace that seemed to fill me with new Life.

I awoke.

My dear cousins, you are not prepared for the sufferings to come. Lose this world now and let its claims on you fall away. If you gain Christ you will lose nothing important.

Not long ago I saw my reflection for the first time in years from a medicine chest in the infirmary. My teeth have rotted and I look decayed. My once hand-some face is etched with grime and lines cut by pain. I look like a corpse straining to draw breath. The doctor gave me hot water to drink for my illness - we have no medicines here. It helped a little.

I felt so sad for myself but was glad my mother was dead. My condition would have killed her. As I headed back to my cell, the Holy Spirit said, *"Don't despair. I will show you as you look to me."*

I suddenly saw my image reflected in the ice. The bumps of the icicles took the lines away and I looked young and alive again. The best part was the snow. It gave the impression that I was dressed in a white robe of righteousness like the saints in heaven wear. It was delightful!

My smiles shock the guards. I can only explain that He is with me.

My dear American cousins, we are praying for you so that when night crashes on your land, and it soon will, your faith will not fail. Put the Cross back in your Gospel-preaching and prepare your people to carry it or they will fall away. It is very cold here. I am praying for a blanket or some rags to keep warm with.

He is with me.

A nameless prisoner,
His ambassador in chains.

Poets, Artists, Musicians, and Dancers

There is a story about Sir Winston Churchill during the dark days of WWII that tells of someone suggesting that the funding for the British Museum be cut and redirected towards the war effort. Though Great Britain was financially strapped, Churchill stood his ground and gave this classic retort, *"No, what do you think we're fighting this war to save?"*

We're taught to revere the memory of God's warriors but His artists are often overlooked. Consider the place and strategic influence of artists in the building of the kingdom of God. God gave a command to Moses in Exodus 31:1-5 — *"I have called by name Bezaleel... and I have filled him with the spirit of God, in wisdom, and in understanding, and in knowledge, and in all manner of workmanship, to devise cunning works..."*

God commissioned an artist - Gasp! He even used his name - to help in the building of his kingdom on earth! The reason that artists are artists and not accountants is that they are artistic. God is the author of creativity, and there are chosen vessels that He sovereignly places His special spark in to create and build works of beauty and grace.

Generally speaking, the more creative someone is, the less likely they are to be practical. Artists don't work well under a 9 to 5 schedule; they do better going with their vision. The ability to see beyond what is and behold what can be with visionary clarity is an exercise in God-honoring faith. It is a creative way of *speaking of those thing which be not as though they were.* Such artist vision is often confused with bragging and arrogance. It is really seeing as present reality what has yet to be created or birthed into this present world. Misunderstood artists often perceive this as a personal curse, but it is a gift from God.

I have a friend who builds houses during the summer. Once

he spent a great deal of time describing in minute detail the latticework on a house he was working on - well, he was planning. When I asked where this beautiful house was, he laughed and tapped his index finger against his head and said, *"In here."* There was no foundation laid, not two boards had been nailed together, yet in his mind, the project was complete. And when summer came, he went and built his dream house. In his mind the thing was done - then came the actual construction.

So many artistic people I know drop out of church because their motivations are so misunderstood. There was a time when God was wooing rock legend Jerry Lee Lewis to himself. He played an aggressive, toe-tapping style of piano. When a pastor heard his music, he summarily threw him out of church. And feeling disillusioned and abandoned by God, he never went back.

How many poets, artists, musicians, and dancers have been thrown out of the church because the church didn't understand them? If you look at the history of so many popular musicians and artists, you'll see an astonishing spiritual legacy in their background and discover that often the church wouldn't make room for them. God promises that our gifts will make room for us, and if the church rejects what we do, the only recourse is to die inside or start working in the world.

I have a godly friend who lives in Nevada and works as a professional dancer. She shakes her head in dismay when people assume she must be some kind of stripper. Equally, too many musicians end up playing in secular bands because there is no room for expression of their art in the community of faith. We're poorer because we reject the soul of the artist - and the devil ends up with all the good music.

Consider the testimony of the artist Bezaleel. The Bible says he was *"filled with the spirit of God, in wisdom, and in understand-*

ing, and in knowledge, and in all manner of workmanship, to devise cunning works…" But wait! If he was really called to serve God, and not his own obvious ego (so the baseless charges go), shouldn't he be teaching Bible studies, or feeding orphans, or doing something, you know, spiritual?

Read the passage and you'll see that God says He gave this man these extraordinary gifts and that He personally called him by name to help build the kingdom of God. Perhaps we would all benefit if we made room for the dreamers and visionaries God raises up. The art in this man's heart would have remained a dream if the church had not rallied and provided him with finances and building materials to create this magnificent work God had called him to build.

A firm confidence in God's calling - be it artistic or not - is not bragging, or vanity, or ego, or any of those trite two-dimensional charges that non-artists inevitability bring. It is creative faith just waiting for a chance to do and be what God breathed it into existence to become.

Hollywood is a perverse force in this world. I can't help but wonder what would happen if we nurtured writers and actors to be salt and light in the entertainment industry instead of accusing them of base, self-serving motives. Perhaps God would anoint their artistic gifts and His kingdom would grow. But no. Let's starve them out, make accusations of their motives, and not support them so they'll fail. I mean, poets, artists, musicians, and dancers really couldn't be of God, could they?'

Cleaning the Cat Box

We used to have a cat. Emphasize *used to*, because I am not a cat lover. We originally got the hair-balled, hair-brained idea of having a cat as a young married couple because we knew we eventually wanted children and figured we needed the practice. It was a flop! Children eventually learn to behave; cats by nature are rebellious.

It's easy to get busy with the everyday issues of living and neglect disliked duties. It's like making a bed. Sure, you do it every morning but begin to wonder why. It will only be rumpled again in a few hours. It's when you start taking domes-tic short-cuts that you find you've stepped into a snare. The messes you've neglect-ed begin to pile higher and higher.

One of my manly household duties was to change the cat box. I remember once gagging at the pungent odor from the box and muttering something about scooping and burying more than just the poop - I was seriously considering taking our obstinate cat out for that long, final ride to the Kitty Corral. Puppies are playful and friendly, birds sing merrily, even ferrets want to romp - but cats sit and stare and pee on the new furniture. They eat expensive plants, too.

One week, I ran a bit lax on cleaning the cat box. The beast had shown no gratitude or affection towards us, her human masters, and I didn't want to be bothered.

Frankly, I had grown a little weary of loving my unlovable cat. It was very early one cool Saturday morning, and I decided to go for a brisk pre-dawn walk. The cat was meowing and scratching but I ignored her.

Kitty had her revenge.

I slipped into some running shorts and a tee shirt. I didn't wear socks because I was trying to build up calluses on my feet; (I'm not a big fan of wearing shoes on the weekend). I grabbed my tennis shoes and bolted for the door. Getting ready for a serious power walk, I dropped my shoes to the ground and slipped my feet in. And my surprised toes hit something gushy and revolting hidden within my left shoe.

Kitty had struck again.

Yep, the cat had decided that the litter box was just too full and disgusting to use, so she chose an alternative dumping ground: my tennis shoes! After the initial wave of revulsion swept over me, I began to seethe and made a quick mental checklist of ways to forever settle the score with the cat.

And then the Holy Spirit convicted me for not loving and caring for my cat. A refrain from Psalms 104:24 began to fill my head. *"O LORD, how manifold are thy works! In wisdom hast thou made them all; the earth is full of thy creatures."*

Oh, yeah. Cats were God's idea.

Goofy as it sounds, I had to repent of my loveless, even homicidal, thoughts towards the cat. After all, I was the one who invited her into my home. I was the guilty one who neglected to empty the cat box. And kitty was merely expressing her opinion of the distasteful situation. Apparently she wasn't happy, either. So I hobbled into the bathroom and gave myself a good foot-washing, and then went and took care of the offending cat box. I gave kitty extra feline treats that morning to a surprising purr of appreciation, and then I went for my walk -barefoot, of course.

There seemed to be a change in attitude on both sides because from that day onward, kitty and I became almost friends. I took care of the cat box and she never unloaded in my shoes again. Of course, I still check the inside of my shoes before putting them on. Just in case.

It's easy to grow weary of doing the right thing day after day. Often we sacrificially love our co-workers and bosses who take advantage of us. We treat with grace and respect those who treat us with contempt. And sometimes we begin to seek short-cuts off of the highway of holiness because we have grown weary. There are times when it's hard to remember that Jesus died for the jerks of this world, too.

Galatians 6:9 — *"And let us not grow weary in well-doing, for in due season we shall reap, if we do not lose heart."* God promises is that if we will surrender ourselves to Him, He will give us the grace to love the loveless, and that we will inherit a blessing from Him, if we faint not. In other words, if we won't quit on doing things God's way, we will receive a blessing from him.

I took a short-cut to serving my cat and she gave me a fetid reminder hidden within my shoe that I was not loving her. And sometimes those unpleasant little surprises we step into are really disguised heart attitude checks from God. Walking in the Spirit often means stepping into the occasional fresh pile of cat doo-doo, and having the contents our hearts exposed before the Lord. What we really are inside is often as disgusting as fresh cat droppings. Thank God for His overcoming Grace!

If you've grown weary in well doing, and you feel like faint-ing, and just want to quit, ask God for a time of refreshing. He is still the God of mercy and comfort and He'll renew you. Or He'll send a cocky cat with an attitude along to help you find a place of repentance and healing.

So when it's your time in life to clean the cat box, or love your loveless neighbor, or to perform whatever unpleasant duty that's beckoning, take heart. You can either inherit a blessing from God or a shoe full of cat fertilizer.

So watch your step!

God of the Outcast

Jeremiah 30:17 — *"For I will restore health to you, and your wounds I will heal, says the LORD, because they have called you an outcast."*

The highways of this fallen world are littered with tossed-off trash — fast food wrappers, exploded tires, unwanted debris, and abandoned wrecks. Dare I include used, forgotten people? An outcast is something that was once regarded as being of value but is now seen as worthless. It's easy to deal with something being an out-cast, but what about when the outcast is a someone?

Consider King David. Here was a young man chosen and anointed of God serving under King Saul. David behaved wisely and the favor of the Lord was upon his life. In I Samuel 18:7, The women sang in the streets, *"Saul has killed his thou-sands, but David his ten thousands."* Jealousy poisoned the old King's dark heart and he began to plot David's death. Having the favor of the Lord often means you must face the envious wrath of man. Could such things happen in the church today? Surely not!

Saul flew into homicidal rages and once nearly pinned David to the wall with a spear. What is a young man of God to do when the King decides to use him for target practice? He finally ran for his life as a refugee and outcast.

God used David's days of running to test him, shape his character and finally place him on the throne of Israel. He started out as a hunted outcast but God destined him for the throne to shepherd His people. It took a rejected, outcast king to fully embrace and love an outcast people.

It is the same for all of God's people. We are seated in heavenly places at the very throne of God. Right now the world may treat us as outcasts and hunt us without mercy but it is we who will one day judge angels, and we shall rule and reign with Christ forever. It is in our times of being outcasts that we learn the ways of Love.

If you find that this world hates you because of your testimony to Christ, know that it hated Him first. The world loves its own; beloved, we are not of this world. We are seeking a city whose builder and maker is God. This present world system hates us because we love Him.

David was an outcast even though he loved God. What of outcasts who have fallen prey to sin? A prostitute once wept on Jesus' feet, kissing them, bathing them with her tears? She even used her hair to dry His feet. And He forgave her sin! Such scandal!

He came to seek and save that which was lost. What would happen if the prostitutes in your town began to find Christ? Would they be welcomed into your church or would they still be treated as fallen outcasts? Religious leaders were shocked that Jesus would allow such a woman to touch Him because in their eyes, when she touched Him, He became unclean, too. Would you have allowed her to touch you?

It often comes down to a single issue: will you be respectable, or will you willingly identify with the outcasts and risk becoming one, too? Who you are willing to love is often a reflection of who you ultimately love, Christ or the world system that hates Him.

When men find buried gold they are honored. What if you went around announcing that you had found hidden treasure in earthen vessels? Imagine honoring and treating with dignity the despised outcasts of this world as God's special possession. Would the church honor or mock you? I've seen both happen.

There was a church that had a formal holiday dinner. The

person who planned the event stated that it was a dress up affair and that if anyone didn't have good clothes, then they should feel bad and not come. It proved to be a gala event and it was all my wife and I could do not to show up in our sweat suits. We were furious at the insensitive gracelessness of it all towards the poor. My response was for all involved to read James chapter 2 concerning the sin of dishonoring the poor in favor of the rich.

Jesus was willingly *"despised, rejected of men,"* because God has a higher way of love that this present world cannot comprehend. That is because Light shines in the darkness and the darkness doesn't comprehend it. In other words, they just don't get it.

God is a Father to the fatherless, a Husband to the widow, the Champion of the poor, the Healer of the brokenhearted, the Savior of sinners. His eyes see value where others only see trash. He is the God who gives beauty for ashes. He is the God of the Outcast.

A Corridor of Portraits

While praying, the Lord opened a beautiful vision to me. I found myself in a very long hallway and at the opposite far end of this hallway was a fireplace burning in a room. I began to walk down the corridor and saw blank canvases hanging in a row. Each was autographed by an artist named Jesus.

Befuddled, I wondered why anyone would hang up empty canvases auto-graphed by the artist as if they were works of genuine art. As I progressed down the hall I began to see a few lines here and there on some of the painting but could not make out any figures or faces.

As I continued down the corridor the paintings began to take shape. I began to see faces and outlines and figures of people. All were lovingly autographed with the signature of Jesus.

At last magnificent charcoal sketches began to appear and I could make out whole faces. These sketches were stunning in their detail and beauty. I kept walking, admiring the black and white masterpieces when suddenly colors began to appear in the paintings. A few splashes of color appeared here and there, and the amount kept increasing with each step. These half-finished paintings were even more haunting in their beauty than the charcoal sketches.

As I neared the end of the corridor the paintings were almost complete. Some merely lacked a few brush strokes, all were indescribably exquisite. The had all been painted by a Master.

Then I entered what I immediately understood to be the family room. There were glorious completed portraits of people from every kindred and tongue, people and nation hanging everywhere. They made up a mural of the grace of God and by comparison, made the Mona Lisa look like bad street graffiti.

Over the roaring hearth was a life-size portrait of Jesus that seemed to glow, lighting up the room. What really struck me was how every painting in the room (and those nearly completed ones in the hall) could look so different from each other but still look like Jesus. There was a definite family resemblance in each portrait to the portrait of Jesus.

As the vision ended, I felt the Holy Spirit quietly ask me a question, *"Child, where would you like your portrait hung?"*

Then I understood the vision. Those at the beginning of the hall were those who had trusted Jesus as Savior but then wouldn't let Him touch them again. The hall represented a picture of people who had progressed to various places of their sanctification and then stopped and refused to go any further with God. Some were hung so close to the family room it was a heartache to see them outside in the corridor. They were almost complete and transformed into the image of Jesus. All the portraits were indeed autographed by Jesus and each was his. Those in the family room were those who had fully yielded their lives by always saying *"Yes"* to Him when He asked - whatever He asked. This is not a picture of salvation by works but of the people bowing their wills to God and walking His narrow way —they had lived their lives to please Him alone.

The Lord was asking me if I would go all the way and let Him paint His masterpiece in me. He calls us to be transformed into the image of His dear Son.

The Christian landscape is littered with what Jesus referred to as half-finished towers, people who started well but then somewhere along the way got hurt, offended, or just began to drift away. The corridor was filled with people who wouldn't go the distance with God.

I looked at the blank canvases, the babes in Christ who wouldn't grow up, and realized that I had indeed let God touch me many times. A holy fear fell on me as I contemplated being hung as a half-finished or even nearly finished masterpiece. Seasons have come when I grew faint and weary with trials and was tempted to just quit.

After seeing the faces of those who had quit in the portraits, I determined anew to run the race set before me, finish the course, and hear, *"Well done, you good and faithful servant."* I want my finished portrait hanging in the family room so I can dwell in the house of the Lord forever.

Child of God, where do you want your portrait hung?

The All-Mushy God?

Genesis 17:1 — *"When Abram was ninety-nine years old the LORD appeared to Abram, and said to him, "I am the All-Mushy God; walk before me, and, though I know you're an absolute slave to sin, just try a little harder -pretty please?"* — The Squirming Flesh Bible, Uncrucified Edition.

Alright, I know that's not at all how the verse reads, but with the way the fluff *gospel* is presented, you'd think someone had rewritten the Holy Book. The verse actually says, Genesis 17:1 — *"When Abram was ninety-nine years old the LORD appeared to Abram, and said to him, "I am God Almighty; walk before me, and be blameless."*

When God gives a command, there comes the divine impartation of grace and power to live that command out in the world. God revealed Himself to Abram as *Almighty* and because of His absolute Might, He commanded Abram to walk before Him and be blameless. Our walking blameless before God does not rest in our ability to work till we can walk blameless before God. Rather it is contingent upon us abiding moment by moment in the presence of the Lord trusting Him to uphold us. It is our relying on His power that allows us to walk blameless before him.

There are two competing *gods* in Christian circles, the All Mushy God, and the Almighty God. One is a pretender and the other is the absolute Lord of all. And which God you bow before and worship will make an eternal difference in your own destiny. So chose wisely.

The Almighty God invites fallen man to new heights in Christ. He offers the opportunity to become new creations in a fallen world. It is He who sees value in prostitutes, deceived religious professors (thank you, Charles Finney), and in outcasts.

He came to invite people such as these into His eternal kingdom. Why, He even loves *good* people! The price of knowing this God is uncompromised love and absolute obedience to His Word and ways. He invites fallen man to cast off his carnal life in order to be raised up and be seated with Him in heavenly places in Christ.

Now consider the All Mushy God. He's the god of the Christian pop culture conferences. He's always contradicting the standards of His Word in favor of a new revelation/new move of the Spirit. He kinda winks at sin because he understands that we are but dust. He knows that we are *only human.*

The All Mushy God cringes at judgmental words like sin, repentance, godly sorrow, and such. He exists only to make men happy and to make us feel good about ourselves. He knows one day we're all going to be gods anyway and wants to stroke our self-esteem. He doesn't demand much of us, just faithful attendance, some money, occasional spiritual activity, and keeping our noses as clean as we can.

Contrast the Almighty God with the All Mushy God. The Almighty is the supreme Creator and Redeemer who came to save men from their sins. The All Mushy God came to sanctify the ego and make good people feel even better about themselves. Might implies great strength. Mush is a goo that just sort of sticks to whatever and requires no backbone. So which "god" are you serving?

The real issue is not in the character of God.

Malachi 3:6 — *"For I the LORD do not change;"* and, Hebrews 13:8 — *"Jesus Christ is the same yesterday and today and for ever."* He is the great I Am.

The problem with the All-Mushy God is that he is a figment of the imagination of deceived men. He is the god we find when we grade on a curve. He is the *dumbed down* God of the Bible. The Almighty God is so lofty and holy that certain pop Bible teachers try to humanize him even as the pagan ancient Greeks did with their lustful, wrathful, petty gods. They diminish His eternal glory and create a fictional god in their own image. And after robbing God of His glory, all that is left is a dumb idol they can peddle for financial gain through their books and tapes in the market place.

The liberating Truth is that God already humanized Himself in the person of Jesus Christ! Phillip asked Jesus to see the Father. And Jesus' classic reply is fitting. John 14:9 — *"Jesus said to him, 'Have I been with you so long, and yet you do not know me, Philip? He who has seen me has seen the Father; how can you say, 'Show us the Father'?"* If you want to see the face of the Almighty God, look into the face of His Son. When you've seen the face of the Son, you've seen the heart of the Father!

We do not need to *dumb down* the Gospel to make the message of the Cross effective and relevant in our modern hip culture. It is only when Jesus is lifted up that He draws men unto Himself.

When you appear before God to give an account of your life, do you expect to see the literal fulfillment of, *"Every knee shall bow and every tongue confess that Jesus is Lord?"* Or do you expect to hear, *"Never mind your numerous adulteries, the children you molested, the thefts and cons you scammed on the unsuspecting,awwwwww gee, I know your heart. Come on in and party, kid."*

Those who serve the Almighty God will joyfully bow the knee and enter into the joy of their Lord. Those who serve the All Mushy God get answer #2 - as the flames are stoked a bit hotter.

Thanking Senōr

While on a recent missions trip to Mexico, I led one of the teams our church sent to show the Campus Crusade for Christ video *JESUS*. We took along a portable video projector and a huge 10 x 14 foot screen. It was like having a portable drive in.

In one gang-infested area, God suddenly laid a message on my heart to the men of the neighborhood. The verse, *"Fear not their faces,"* was ringing in my heart. The smell of marijuana was thick over this dark and oppressed neighborhood and we were too far from the border to make a successful run for it. It was one of those nights when it came down to really trusting God. Oh no, was it really down to that?!

Obeying the prompting of the Holy Spirit, I began preaching through a brave 15-year-old interpreter, while standing in a pile of manure no less, that Jesus was the real man to emulate. I began preaching against wife beating, pornography, alcohol abuse and marijuana. I challenged the men of the neighborhood to look to Jesus as the example of what a man was to be. Look to Jesus to see that men should loves their wives and children. Under my breath, I was also praying that God would convict these men that real men don't shoot missionaries, but with my gift of wisdom working in full gear, I figured I ought not speak that one publicly! And God came.

A great number of people came forward at the end of the film and repented and prayed to meet Christ. It was a powerful night; what a demonstration of the power of simply preaching Christ and Him crucified. The word of God convicted many and several men came forward, some drunk, to pray and repent of their lives of sin.

When we were finished, we packed the vehicle and departed to the cheers of smiling neighborhood kids. I felt great! Our driver Tom suggested that we thank Senōr for the marvelous job He did ministering. I beamed with pride and said in all humility, *"It was a team effort. You're welcome."* And the van got very quiet until Tom started chortling.

It turns out that Senōr is the title of respect they use for Jesus!

Anyway, there are moments when God will come along and sort of prick your heart to see what bleeds out. I felt pretty stupid. The truth is that the team really did perform fantastically. Our *ministry of helps* technical crew became very efficient in short order. Our oversized film screen was a nightmare to negotiate with when the wind was blowing. Yet we worked together and overcame all obstacles, doing as God directed us to do, and the result was that a great many Mexicans came to faith in Christ.

Through this, I saw with marvel and clarity the need for all members of the Body of Christ to be functioning in harmony with the head (Jesus) and with each other. Often we exult the preachers and speakers because they have the public eye. But without the administrators, the helps, the *fill-in-the-blankers*, the Gospel would not go forth.

For years I served as a sound-man in church. It was the most difficult ministry and I was grateful to be finally paroled! I did my time. Facing a gang-infested neighborhood crowned with green marijuana smoke is one thing, but try working service after service dealing with angry people, some who claim the sound is too loud while others complain that they can't hear. Try recording a special service only to find the tape has a manufacturer's defect and nothing is recorded. And it's always the sound-man's (or secretary, or janitor, or nursery worker's) fault.

Loving God is easy. It's loving people that finally makes or breaks your faith. Instead of focusing on human performance, on human success and failure, perhaps we could all simply bow our heads and Thank Senõr for the wonders he has wrought. It would cure a lot of strife among believers.

So, Thank You, Senõr, for using us in spite of ourselves. To You alone be all glory, honor, and power. We're honored to be co-laborers with you as your Gospel goes forth into the nations.

Personal

Bryan & Cyndi Hupperts married in 1989. They have two children. They ran a campus ministry together ministering to international students attending Southeast Missouri State University in Cape Girardeau, MO. They are now launching SheepTrax Media.™

Cyndi is a marketing professional with an extensive background in all aspects of advertising. She was raised in a conservative Buddhist home in Kuala Lumpur, Malaysia and received Christ at age 13. Bryan is a native St. Louisan. He was raised Roman Catholic and received Christ on his 18th birthday after listening to an album by the late Keith Green of *Last Days Ministries*.

The Hupperts attend World View Community Church in St. Louis, MO.

Vision Statement of SheepTrax Media

SheepTrax Media™ is an evangelistic and prophetic publishing and new media company. We e-publish SheepTrax Digest, the *"wit, wisdom, and deepthinking"* of Christian humorist, musician, speaker, and writer Bryan Hupperts. We also publish witnessing tracts, Bryan's one-act plays, and the SheepTrax Devotional book series.

Bryan's work has appeared in numerous magazines, including Church Growth Magazine, a publication of Yoido Full Gospel Church, South Korea. He was recently interviewed by Charisma Magazine, and frequently appears as a guest on radio programs.

Bryan writes and performs quirky original songs with titles like, *Adam Didn't Eat Bananas, Dial Some 900 Psychic, Country Goth Chick, Cancel That Trip To Graceland!*, and *I Got A Spanking From Santa*. He also performs original folk/pop style ballads.

He seeks to minister to secularized, postmoderns packaging truth in culturally relevant ways. He is available for conferences, concerts, and events. As a former campus pastor, he is especially at home on college and university campuses and welcomes the opportunity to help harvest your campus for Jesus.

For booking information, please contact:

Bryan Hupperts
SheepTrax Media
PO Box 270256
St. Louis, MO 63127 USA
(314) 416-0958
deepsheep@sheeptrax.com
www.SheepTrax.com

Subscribe to SheepTrax Digest at deepsheep@sheeptrax.com. Yes, it's free!

Impact Christian Books

332 Leffingwell Ave., Suite 101
Kirkwood, MO 63122

AVAILABLE AT YOUR LOCAL BOOKSTORE, OR YOU MAY
ORDER DIRECTLY. Toll-Free, order-line only M/C, DISC,
or VISA 1-800-451-2708.

Visit our Website at *www. impactchristianbooks.com*

Write for *FREE* Catalog.

Recommended Web Pages

SheepTrax Media
www.SheepTrax.com
http://groups.yahoo.com/group/SheepTrax

World View Community Church
Tom & Mary Helbig, pastors
http://www.worldviewcommunity.com

David & Kathie Walters
Youth Evangelists
http://www.goodnews.netministries.org

Storm-Harvest Ministries
Robert Holmes - Australia
http://www.storm-harvest.asn.au

Impact Christian Books
Our humble publisher, Bill Banks
http://www.impactchristianbooks.com

Jack Whitney Studio
Digital Illustration, Animation & Design
Jack designed both our logo and the cover artwork
http://www.jwhitneystudio.com